STUDIES IN MOTION

STUDIES IN MOTION

The Hauntings of Eadweard Muybridge

A Play in Two Acts

SECOND EDITION

Kevin Kerr

Talonbooks

Talonbooks
P.O. Box 2076, Vancouver, British Columbia, Canada v6b 3s3
www.talonbooks.com

Typeset in Frutiger and printed and bound in Canada
Printed on 100% post-consumer recycled paper
Typeset and cover design by Typesmith

First printing, second edition: 2013

Talonbooks gratefully acknowledges the financial support of the Canada Council
for the Arts, the Government of Canada through the Canada Book Fund, and the
Province of British Columbia through the British Columbia Arts Council, and the
Book Publishing Tax Credit.

Rights to produce *Studies in Motion*, in whole or in part, in any medium by any
group, amateur or professional, are retained by the author. Interested persons are
requested to apply to him care of Talonbooks.

Images of Eadweard Muybridge motion studies used courtesy of Flickr,
released under Creative Commons 2.0 by the Boston Public Library.
http://www.flickr.com/photos/boston_public_library

LIBRARY AND ARCHIVES CANADA CATALOGUING IN PUBLICATION

Kerr, Kevin, 1968–, author
    Studies in motion : the hauntings of Eadweard Muybridge /
Kevin Kerr. — 2nd edition.

A play.
Issued in print and electronic formats.
ISBN 978-0-88922-810-8.—ISBN 978-0-88922-811-5 (epub)

    1. Muybridge, Eadweard, 1830–1904—Drama. I. Title.

PS8571.E719S89 2013   C812'.6   C2013-901932-4

For Marita

One never understands anything from a photograph ...
Only that which narrates can make us understand.

– SUSAN SONTAG

Studies in Motion: The Hauntings of Eadweard Muybridge (2006), Electric Company Theatre.
PHOTOS BY Tim Matheson

DESIGN-BASED DRAMATURGY

The work of Eadweard Muybridge was a critical part of a revolution in how people would think about motion, vision, and the power of technology to unlock truth hidden from our fallible natural senses. His work foretold the advent of cinema and in part gave birth to our modern visual age. Muybridge was an innovator, not because he strove to innovate, but because his obsessive pursuit of an idea that had no precedent forced him to invent new ways of work and of seeing.

The path to creating *Studies in Motion* is another example of the innovative creative process, this time with Electric Company Theatre, where the writing of the script is an interactive exchange with directorial vision, staging, design, technology, and performance. All scripts are blueprints for a future production, but in the case of Electric Company, they are also an incomplete record of a collaborative investigation into an idea – often one without precedent.

The company was founded with the goal of creating original theatre rooted in visual and physical imagery, with a strong sense of story. Cinematic vocabulary is a critical component of the company's aesthetic, and our incorporation of the language of cinema into our work in various ways has been an ongoing investigation. This story, of an obsessive, mysterious creator living at the frontiers of both the American West and of photographic advancement, who would accelerate the invention of the motion picture, was a natural subject for us to explore.

After pitching the idea of a play about Muybridge to Kim Collier and Jonathon Young, my collaborators at Electric Company, we began envisioning a piece that would be in part a celebration of the human body onstage – a piece that was a dance between text, narrative, staging, and choreography. We were excited to imagine theatrical representations of Muybridge's dissection of time and motion, recreating live the stroboscopic qualities of cinema and the persistence of vision, and began to investigate how to achieve that.

Serendipitously we were approached by a past collaborator, Robert Gardiner, a celebrated designer and professor at the University of British Columbia's department of theatre, who was exploring through the support of a Social Sciences and Humanities Research Council grant the use of digital lighting projectors to replace traditional theatre lighting instruments and create a comprehensive digital scenography. His ideas involved using the projectors to light the stage; create locations with projected environments, textures, and animations; and interact with the performers. It was a way of thinking of design as a part of the "text" of the play, and the innovative nature of both the concept and of the technology was reminiscent of Muybridge's experiments with instantaneous photography.

Conversations among Kim, Jonathon, Robert, and myself spurred the early development of the piece. And critical to its creation were a series of physical workshops hosted by the theatre department at UBC.

Led by Kim Collier, the workshops would combine the script in progress with experiments in staging and the use of the projectors as the central design element. Kim assembled a cast of actors, including Jonathon, who is a particularly gifted physical actor and was also able to respond to the script's development from within the world of the play. As well, Kim brought together the other integral players in the production, including internationally renowned choreographer Crystal Pite (Kidd Pivot), who joined Kim to create beautiful movement and dance sequences and other physical units that were written into the script. These were not only aesthetically rich and captivating passages, but they were integral to the telling of the story. At the same time, composer Patrick Pennefather would respond to the physical work he was seeing onstage by bringing in new pieces of music daily. His electronic and very modern sounding score reflected the technologically groundbreaking work Muybridge was doing with his photography. While this was happening, costume designer Mara Gottler would be conducting experiments with fabric to determine how different materials would respond to the digital light sources, which have a very different quality than incandescent theatrical lighting instruments. She also had to solve the problem of getting actors from being onstage completely nude to full Victorian dress in a matter of seconds. Holding it all together was stage manager Jan Hodgson, who created systems of coordinating and executing an evolving show that would contain hundreds upon hundreds of cues and a half-dozen operators in control of individual elements.

Throughout this process, I would bring in new ideas for scenes as well as take away inspiration from the work being done in the room to write various drafts between workshops and prior to production. Having learned enormous amounts from the physical process, I could write with a better of idea of how the elements would interact and know which things might be achievable and which would not. I would work closely with Kim and Jonathon in dramaturgical sessions to figure out the structure of the script and address questions of which parts of the story were in the words, which were in the design, and which were in the bodies in motion onstage.

After the show premiered in Vancouver at the PuSh International Performing Arts Festival in 2006, there were extensive rewrites incorporating everything we learned from the full production. We toured the revised version of the script to the Yukon Arts Centre, Vancouver Playhouse, Alberta Theatre Projects, and Festival TransAmériques in Montreal. But every production is a chance to discover, and there were still things about the piece that we weren't entirely satisfied with.

A co-production of the play between Canadian Stage Company in Toronto and the Citadel Theatre in Edmonton provided an opportunity to tackle questions around the drive of the play and the balance between the stories of Muybridge's relationship with Flora and his obsessive investigation of animal locomotion more than a decade later. In this process Canadian Stage artistic director Matthew Jocelyn joined in on our company dramaturgical sessions and added his wisdom to the mix. Given the intricate structure of the piece, each change would often result in a ripple of changes moving back and forth through the script, so the revisions were extensive. But it resulted in a more dynamic and energized story and further enhanced the interplay among text, staging, and design.

This preface is itself an incomplete transcript of a process, which is never truly complete, for theatre, a living and breathing animal, is always an investigation that remains in motion.

KEVIN KERR

Studies in Motion was first produced by Electric Company Theatre in partnership with Theatre at UBC and the PuSh International Performing Arts Festival in performance at the Frederic Wood Theatre in Vancouver between January 17 and 29, 2006, with the following artistic team:

EADWEARD MUYBRIDGE	Andrew Wheeler
RONDINELLA / ROYAL SOCIETY MAN ONE / RULOFSON	Ryan Beil
FLORA, MOTHER ON STREET	Lara Gilchrist
FLOREDO	Kai James
BIGLER	Shane Kolmansberger
STANFORD / PEPPER / BLACKSMITH / FOREMAN	Allan Morgan
SUSAN / CRIB PLAYER ONE	Dawn Petten
TADD / DERELICT	Joel Redmond
BELL / COPPINGER / ROYAL SOCIETY MAN TWO	Kyle Rideout
BLANCHE	Juno Ruddell
SISTER ANNE-MARIE / ACTRESS / MRS. SMITH / CRIB PLAYER TWO	Erin Wells
LARKYNS / EAKINS / ROYAL SOCIETY MAN THREE	Jonathon Young

Director	Kim Collier
Scenographer	Robert Gardiner
Choreographer	Crystal Pite
Costume Designer	Mara Gottler
Composer and Sound Designer	Patrick Pennefather
Stage Manager	Jan Hodgson

A revised version premiered at the Yukon Arts Centre in March 25 to 27, 2009, as part of a multicity tour that included the Vancouver Playhouse, Alberta Theatre Projects (Calgary), and Festival TransAmérique (Montreal), with the following artistic team:

EADWEARD MUYBRIDGE	Andrew Wheeler
BLANCHE	Juno Ruddell
FLORA	Anastasia Phillips
LARKYNS / EAKINS	Jonathon Young
STANFORD / PEPPER / BLACKSMITH	Allan Morgan
SUSAN	Dawn Petten
BELL	Kyle Rideout
TADD	Gaelan Beatty
BIGLER	Kristian Ayre
RONDINELLA	Josh Epstein
MRS. HARRISON / ACTRESS / NURSE	Erin Wells
FLOREDO	Julien Galipeau

Director	Kim Collier
Original Scenographer and Media	Robert Gardiner
Choreographer	Crystal Pite
Costume Designer	Mara Gottler
Composer	Patrick Pennefather
Stage Manager	Jan Hodgson
Additional Lighting Designer	Adrian Muir
Assistant Stage Manager	Jennifer Swan
Assistant Scenographer	Jamie Nesbitt
Rehearsal Movement Director	Andrea Hodge
Assistant Director	Blake William Turner

The updated version of the play published here premiered October 30 to November 14, 2010, at the Citadel Theatre in Edmonton as a co-production with Canadian Stage Company in Toronto, where it played November 25 to December 18, 2010, with the following artistic team:

EADWEARD MUYBRIDGE	Andrew Wheeler
BLANCHE	Juno Ruddell
FLORA	Celine Stubbel
LARKYNS / EAKINS	Jonathon Young
STANFORD / PEPPER / BLACKSMITH	Allan Morgan
SUSAN	Dawn Petten
BELL	Kyle Rideout
TADD	Gaelan Beatty
BIGLER	Mike Rinaldi
RONDINELLA	Frank Zotter
MRS. HARRISON / ACTRESS / NURSE	Erin Wells
FLOREDO	Julien Galipeau

Director	Kim Collier
Original Scenographer and Media	Robert Gardiner
Choreographer	Crystal Pite
Costume Designer	Mara Gottler
Composer	Patrick Pennefather
Stage Manager	Jan Hodgson
Additional Lighting Designer	Adrian Muir
Assistant Stage Manager	Jennifer Swan
Assistant Scenographer	Jamie Nesbitt
Rehearsal Movement Director	Andrea Hodge
Assistant Director	Blake William Turner

CAST OF CHARACTERS

(in order of appearance)

Models
Eadweard Muybridge
Royal Society Man One
Royal Society Man Two
Royal Society Man Three
Derelict (Londoner)
Londoners
Leland Stanford, *a Californian railroad magnate*
Dr. William Pepper, *University of Pennsylvania provost*
L.F. Rondinella, *camera operator*
William Bigler, *head of electrics*
Henry Bell, *darkroom technician*
J. Liberty Tadd, *model wrangler*
Thomas Eakins, *an art college instructor*
Blanche, *a volunteer at the photography compound*
Susan, *a model*
Sister Anne-Marie
Floredo Muybridge
Jury Members
Flora Muybridge
Blacksmith, *a reluctant model*
Mrs. Harrison, *a concerned citizen*
Henry Larkyns, *a theatre critic*
Coppinger, *Henry's ghostwriter*
An Actress
Mrs. Smith, *a nurse*
Rulofson, *Muybridge's business associate*
Crib Player One, *a sporting lady*
Crib Player Two, *a modern woman*
Jury Foreman

ABOUT MUYBRIDGE'S PHOTOGRAPHIC TECHNIQUE

A great deal of action in the play revolves around Muybridge's investigation into "human and animal locomotion." To help the reader visualize what the process of taking his motion study photographs entailed, I'll attempt to describe the physical reality of how he worked.

Muybridge photographed the majority of his subjects moving along the length of a track set up outdoors on the grounds of the University of Pennsylvania. Subjects moved in front of a white backdrop painted with grid lines so that any change in position, from image to image, could be somewhat accurately measured.

Facing the backdrop, he set up a battery of either twelve or twenty-four cameras. The cameras were essentially just one large rectangular wooden box with the twelve or twenty-four lenses lined up in a row along the front. Inside, the box was subdivided into as many chambers as lenses, each with its own spring-loaded shutter. A glass plate, coated in light-sensitive emulsion, was brought from the "darkroom" (an on-site tent that had been completely blacked out) inside an opaque shield to keep it protected from the light. The shield was dropped into the back of the camera, the plate released, and the shield then withdrawn so that the glass could receive the image when the shutter was sprung. After the photograph was taken, the glass plate was removed from the camera, again using the opaque shield, and rushed to the tent to be processed. The shutters were triggered by an electric signal sent by a timing device so that each camera would fire sequentially in a steady rhythm. This rhythm could be sped up for fast actions and slowed down for slower actions so that the twenty-four photographs could be taken in a fraction of a second or over several seconds.

For many series, Muybridge employed an additional battery of cameras positioned to view the subject from behind as they moved down the track away from the cameras. A third set of cameras was set up to view the subject from the front and was positioned at a forty-five degree angle to the track. The three sets of cameras were all connected to the same timing device so that the cameras would fire in unison, ensuring that every frame from each angle would represent the exact same moment of time.

The technology was new (much of it of Muybridge's own devising) and prone to malfunction. The process was time consuming, weather dependent, and subject to the unpredictable nature of animals and human volunteers in a highly charged environment.

SETTING

The play takes place in two locations and time periods: (1) northern California in the early 1870s; and (2) Muybridge's outdoor photography compound at the University of Pennsylvania in 1885, with occasional stops elsewhere. The play flows fluidly between these two times and places.

A NOTE ON OVERLAPPING DIALOGUE

Occasionally characters in the play speak overtop one another. A "/" inside a character's speech indicates the point where the next character begins speaking, with the first character continuing through to the end of their line. If a line of dialogue that is marked with a "/" contains no punctuation at the end, it means that character continues speaking overtop the interrupting voice through to their next speech without pause.

ACT ONE
The World to a Bullet

PRESHOW
||||||||||||||||||||||||||||||

> *An empty stage delineated by a grid – a mathematical sense of space and time.*
>
> *Projection (image): Face of Eadweard Muybridge*
>
> *Muybridge's intense, staring eyes survey the audience as they enter.*
>
> *Lights fade. The face disappears.*

PROLOGUE
||||||||||||||||||||||||||||||

> *A gunshot. Music. Far upstage a nude man walks rhythmically across the stage. A second nude man walks the same journey. A nude man runs the length of the stage. Another man sprints across. Two men run in close proximity. A man runs, jumps high into the air, lands, and continues his run.*
>
> *A nude woman walks across the stage. Another nude woman flutters a fan as she walks across the stage. A woman hops on one foot. A woman runs across the stage. Two women walk towards each other, meet, and kiss. Another woman skips rope.*
>
> *A little clothing is added.*
>
> *A man points a rifle. Another man swings a pickaxe. Two men wrestle.*
>
> *Wearing a diaphanous skirt or dress, a woman twirls. Another woman does a dance step. Yet another woman brushes her hair.*
>
> *A fully clothed man wearing a boater hat and carrying a cane struts across the stage, pivots on one foot, and returns the way he came.*

[1]

Another man in Victorian clothes leapfrogs over the shoulders of another man.

A pair of men perform cartwheels.

Two men approach each other and shake hands.

A woman carries a bucket of water.

A woman in Victorian dress leaps over a chair.

A woman beats another woman with a broom.

A woman carries a parasol; a man passes her and tips his hat.

Thunderclap.

The world of the motion study is suddenly broken as rain starts to fall. The two look up. The man offers the woman his arm and they run for cover.

ROYAL SOCIETY
||||||||||||||||||||||||||||||||||||||||||

Projection (text): London, 1884

Thunder. Pissing rain. MUYBRIDGE enters surveying the street, while checking the address written on a scrap of paper. He finds what he is looking for and moves towards his destination.

The sound of rain fades and we are suddenly inside the Royal Society. MUYBRIDGE puts his gear down and removes his dripping jacket. The three men, directors of the Royal Society, fix him in an icy stare.

MUYBRIDGE
I beg your pardon. Cats and dogs. Cats and dogs.

ROYAL SOCIETY MAN ONE
And horses.

MUYBRIDGE
Eh?

ROYAL SOCIETY MAN ONE
Horses too.

MUYBRIDGE is momentarily nonplussed.

MUYBRIDGE
Uh ... right. I apologize for being –

They each hold a copy of an identical book.

ROYAL SOCIETY MAN TWO
Might we assume that this was to be the subject of tonight's lecture?

ROYAL SOCIETY MAN ONE
Horses!

ROYAL SOCIETY MAN TWO
Horse manure more like it.

*MUYBRIDGE takes a copy of the book from
ROYAL SOCIETY MAN ONE.*

MUYBRIDGE
Uh ... I ... pardon? Where did you get this?

ROYAL SOCIETY MAN TWO
This is the Royal Society of London. We have a curious habit of keeping
abreast of things.

ROYAL SOCIETY MAN THREE
The title of this book is *The Horse in Motion* by – are you listening? –
J.D.B. Stillman, M.D. I'm aware that your name has a tendency to
change from time to time. I don't suppose it recently changed
to J.D.B. Stillman, did it?

ROYAL SOCIETY MAN TWO
M.D.?

ROYAL SOCIETY MAN ONE
Horses.

MUYBRIDGE
That is my work ... that is –

ROYAL SOCIETY MAN THREE
By J.D.B. Stillman ... under the auspices of Leland Stanford.

MUYBRIDGE
No, this is a mistake ...

ROYAL SOCIETY MAN THREE
I don't think it's a typo. It's embossed ... in gold ... on the cover:
J.D.B. Stillman –

ROYAL SOCIETY MAN TWO
M.D.

MUYBRIDGE
These are my photographs.

ROYAL SOCIETY MAN THREE
Yes, well, to your credit, under "Acknowledgements to Technical Staff" –

ROYAL SOCIETY MAN TWO
You'll find it at the back.

ROYAL SOCIETY MAN THREE
you are listed –

ROYAL SOCIETY MAN TWO
Pretty near the bottom.

ROYAL SOCIETY MAN THREE
as a "skilled photographer."

ROYAL SOCIETY MAN ONE
Horses.

ROYAL SOCIETY MAN TWO
And you're travelling Europe advertising someone else's research as your own.

MUYBRIDGE
No, no, no. But this *is* my work. This *is* my research.

ROYAL SOCIETY MAN TWO
Or so you have led all of Europe to believe.

MUYBRIDGE
This ... I'm ... Well, this looks ... But ... Surely you're aware ... In France, I was ...

ROYAL SOCIETY MAN THREE
This is England, that was France.

ROYAL SOCIETY MAN ONE
I see Eadweard's underpants.

MUYBRIDGE
What?

ROYAL SOCIETY MAN ONE
You're not who you say you are!

ROYAL SOCIETY MAN TWO
We're not like the rest of your dupes.

MUYBRIDGE
I have a paper –

ROYAL SOCIETY MAN THREE

Your presentation has been cancelled. Your "work" will not be accepted at the Royal Society.

MUYBRIDGE

But –

ROYAL SOCIETY MAN TWO

Fraud.

ROYAL SOCIETY MAN THREE

You are excused.

ROYAL SOCIETY MAN ONE

... and the horse you rode in on!

A door slams like thunder.

BOOK DANCE
|||||||||||||||||||||||||||||||||||||||

> *The men are gone and we are outside on the street. Copies of the Stillman book pour down like heavy rain. MUYBRIDGE is devastated and in shock. People hurriedly pass by in the downpour. A rough-looking man walks by MUYBRIDGE.*

DERELICT

(*without breaking stride*) Murderer.

> *The crowd stops.*

MUYBRIDGE

What? What? What did you say to me?

> *The man is gone. MUYBRIDGE stands flustered as he feels people staring at him. MUYBRIDGE picks up a copy of the book and throws it offstage after the man. MUYBRIDGE collapses in a heap.*

> *The crowd tentatively approaches the scattered books and, as rain continues to drive down, one by one they pick them up and place them over their heads for cover. They begin to dance. MUYBRIDGE doesn't participate and, partway through, he trudges offstage. At the end of the movement sequence, one man remains. It is Leland STANFORD.*

Projection (text): San Francisco, 1884

MUYBRIDGE storms on and presents the contentious book.

MUYBRIDGE
What is the meaning of this?

STANFORD
It's a book about horses.

MUYBRIDGE
It's theft.

STANFORD
Of what?

MUYBRIDGE
Of my work ... my photographs.

STANFORD
I'm sorry? *Whose* photographs?

MUYBRIDGE
My –

STANFORD
No, no. *Whose* photographs? Where did the money come from?
Who paid for this? Who?

MUYBRIDGE
Sir, Mr. Stanford, you can't own the creative –

STANFORD
I didn't hear the answer! The cameras, the staff, the track, the fucking
horses, they were mine. Weren't they? Am I crazy?

MUYBRIDGE
Yes, but the photographs –

STANFORD
The book is not about making photographs – the photographs are
incidental – the book is about science.

MUYBRIDGE
The photographs *are* the science. The photographs are the story!
Stillman / would be speaking in a vacuum if

STANFORD
No, no, no, no, don't you – no.

MUYBRIDGE
there were no photographs. Where was he when the work was being done? His commentary, / his annotation

STANFORD
Where was he? Where were *you* when he wrote this? It's two separate things.

MUYBRIDGE
his banal and uninspired notes in the margin of my – where was *I*? (*pointing at the photos*) I'm right here. And here. And / here; in the pictures.

STANFORD
And he's right here and here and here / in the words!

MUYBRIDGE
I created all of that, and he has simply signed his name to what is mine.

STANFORD
NO!

MUYBRIDGE
YES!

STANFORD
NO!

MUYBRIDGE
MINE!

STANFORD
MINE!

     Pause.

MUYBRIDGE
I would hate to take legal action.

STANFORD
What?

     MUYBRIDGE adjusts his jacket.

STANFORD
I beg your pardon?

MUYBRIDGE

I don't want to have to –

STANFORD

You want to go court? Trust me you don't. You do that and I will crush you – I will absolutely fucking destroy you. Sir.

> *Defeated, MUYBRIDGE begins to leave, but suddenly spins back on STANFORD.*

MUYBRIDGE

Sir, do you really believe that book is the summation of our ten years' work? If so, then you've missed what we've really done. What *I've* really done. I've stopped time. I've found out how to see the truth. And knowing that all four hooves are off the ground is far less interesting than knowing that we can now know it. For you, this was the last picture; for me, it is the first. The veil is about to be drawn back; pity your short-sightedness will leave you looking the other way.

FRESH START
||||||||||||||||||||||||||||||||||||||||

> *Projection (text):* University of Pennsylvania, 1885

> *Outdoors on campus, a group of men move into the space setting up cameras, measuring distances, focusing lenses, running cables. In the midst of the action is MUYBRIDGE. He looks up to see the university's provost, Dr. William Pepper, enter.*

MUYBRIDGE

Dr. Pepper!

PEPPER

Muybridge!

MUYBRIDGE

(*to the men*) Provost of the university. (*back to PEPPER*) Everything is in excellent order. Meet the team: L.F. Rondinella, chief of staff and principal camera operator.

RONDINELLA

We've got twenty-four cameras in sequence to capture movement along the lateral plane.

MUYBRIDGE

Place another dozen from behind and –

RONDINELLA

Done! And another twelve looking from the front.

MUYBRIDGE

Yes! William A. Bigler, head of electrics.

BIGLER

The cameras are now synchronized as requested. Camera one here will fire at the same instant as camera one back there and over there.

MUYBRIDGE

Good! For the first time the photographer is not tied to his physical position in space. We see the subject from here and here and here all at the exact same moment. I've stopped time and now I've eliminated space.

BIGLER

(*in awe*) You don't even have to pay me to be here, you know.

MUYBRIDGE

Henry Bell, darkroom operations.

BELL

We have enough silver nitrate prepared to make more than ten thousand photographs.

MUYBRIDGE

Then double it.

BELL

Oh, I'm sorry, no, that's just what I've prepped for the animals. For the human studies I've got enough for another fifty thousand.

MUYBRIDGE

Well done, son!

>   *They shake hands.*

MUYBRIDGE

Good grip! What's your sport?

BELL

Baseball, rowing, shot put, wrestling, and the sprint!

MUYBRIDGE

Yes! And J. Liberty Tadd, artist and model wrangler.

TADD

I've got full clearance from the veterinary school next door that we can use their animals.

MUYBRIDGE

Excellent! Start with the horses, other domesticated livestock, and look into wild beasts. What about humans?

TADD

There's a bit of confusion.

MUYBRIDGE

Which is?

TADD

How will the models be dressed?

MUYBRIDGE

How will the animals be dressed?

TADD

Sir?

MUYBRIDGE

Make sure Mr. Bell is on your roster! A fine specimen.

PEPPER

So you're satisfied with the facilities?

MUYBRIDGE

The university has been most accommodating.

PEPPER

Good, we have somewhere to be.

> *MUYBRIDGE leads PEPPER away and the photography compound disappears behind them.*

MUYBRIDGE

Where's that?

PEPPER

Reception.

MUYBRIDGE

I'm not suited to those types of situations.

PEPPER

It's not optional. These are the funders of the university. It's their privilege to rub shoulders with you.

MUYBRIDGE
I'm not dressed for it.

PEPPER
They'll love it. It's character. You're a celebrity.

MUYBRIDGE falters. PEPPER quickly clarifies his point.

PEPPER
I mean with your pictures.

MUYBRIDGE
I'm here to work.

PEPPER
You're here because we're paying for it.

MUYBRIDGE
I'm paying for it. Through the subscriptions to the catalogue.

PEPPER
Any subscribers yet?

MUYBRIDGE
There will be subscribers.

PEPPER
Come to the reception. Sell them on the idea. We need to convince
these people how it's going to advance my mission for the University
of Pennsylvania. To become a leader in research and applied sciences.

MUYBRIDGE
You can convince them.

PEPPER
No, I can't.

MUYBRIDGE
Why not?

PEPPER
Because I don't have the language to describe all that you're doing.

MUYBRIDGE
Well, it's very clear. Through to end of summer I intend to complete
the most exhaustive investigation into animal locomotion ever
known. I will photograph the movements of not only horses, domestic
animals, and wild beasts, but men and women as well in all of their
possible postures, actions, and activities. The results I believe will be

an invaluable resource to scientists, doctors, and artists, as I seek to do what no one has attempted before: to make the invisible seen, and the intangible qualities of our ever-accelerating world at last perceptible.

The scene shifts.

RECEPTION
||||||||||||||||||||||||||||||||

> *They are at the reception and a crowd of well-to-do men and women applaud MUYBRIDGE's speech. They break and begin to mingle. PEPPER pats MUYBRIDGE on the back.*

PEPPER
See? That was great! Oh!

> *PEPPER points to EAKINS, the art instructor, who is in the distance eating a rolled-up pancake and chatting with some guests.*

PEPPER
Thomas Eakins. Eakins!

> *PEPPER catches the eye of EAKINS, who bounds over. PEPPER gestures to him in introduction. A series of handshakes.*

PEPPER
Eakins.

EAKINS
Eakins. Thomas Eakins. Bill.

PEPPER
Tommy. (*referring to rolled-up pancake*) Where did you get that?

EAKINS
(*points*) Trolley.

PEPPER
I'll be back.

> *PEPPER chases down the food trolley.*

EAKINS
I loved the presentation. I'm very excited about this project. Very excited.

MUYBRIDGE
Good.

EAKINS

I've been a principal supporter. A backroom player.

EAKINS suddenly touches MUYBRIDGE – rubs his arm, places a hand on his abdomen.

EAKINS

You're in incredible shape.

MUYBRIDGE

Yes, well ...

EAKINS

Ah, I beg your pardon. I'm a tremendous fan of the human body. I'm the head of instruction at the academy. Drawing and painting, you know?

A woman, MRS. HARRISON, walks up to EAKINS and slaps his face. She exits. There's a pause in which neither man opts to address what just happened. EAKINS eventually picks up the ball.

EAKINS

You're by the veterinary school, yes?

MUYBRIDGE

Yes.

EAKINS

That's convenient.

PEPPER returns with food.

PEPPER

He needs humans.

EAKINS

Oh, I have models – I teach a life class.

MUYBRIDGE

Yes?

PEPPER

Where did Mrs. Harrison go? I want to introduce her to Ed.

MUYBRIDGE

Eadweard.

PEPPER

She's currently the money behind your project. I just saw her a second ago.

EAKINS
I think she left.

PEPPER
I'll bring her by sometime.

EAKINS
Say, do you mind if I come by while you work? I think you and I are –

He makes a gesture indicating that they're on the same wavelength.

PEPPER
Tommy's a photographer as well.

MUYBRIDGE
Oh?

EAKINS
I'm an amateur. But it's transformed the way I paint.

PEPPER
Don't sell yourself short. He's inspired.

MUYBRIDGE
Undoubtedly. You think you could enlist some female models?

PEPPER
Oh, is it girls too?

EAKINS
You bet. They're not educated – but they're uninhibited and I think that's what you're asking.

PEPPER
What will they be doing?

EAKINS
Posing, fool.

MUYBRIDGE
No. Moving. Specific to their sex.

EAKINS
See, it's exactly what I'm interested in. For centuries woman have been just lying around in art. Why? Because the form is beautiful? Sure. But really, the fact is, it's easier than trying to paint someone walking by. But with what you're proposing ... I swear, you've been reading my journals.

MUYBRIDGE

I've been working on this for a decade.

EAKINS

I'll be your partner.

MUYBRIDGE

I don't need a partner – though I'm honoured – but I do need female models.

EAKINS

I can get them by the bushel.

PEPPER

He's got the magic touch.

MUYBRIDGE

Well, I've not photographed women in this manner before, so your assistance would be invaluable.

EAKINS

The motivation is purely selfish. I'm fascinated by what we can discover. This is your Noah's ark – all the animals safely preserved in the display of their basic primal actions. All safe from the coming flood.

The sound of rushing water is heard as the scene shifts.

THE RIVER

The river flows serenely by. BLANCHE sits sketching the scenery. She stops, looks at what she's done, and attempts to fix it, but the sketch only gets worse as she tries to reconcile the mess.

BLANCHE

Well, Father, I suppose you're in heaven now looking down on me and shaking your head. It's supposed to be Ophelia floating away on the river, but it's so ugly it would drive Shakespeare to suicide. I hope you're satisfied. The truth is, I don't have the slightest clue what I'm doing. No, the truth is, Father, we just made a really good team. Maybe it should be me floating away in the river to be with you again.

She crumples up the sketch.

> *A noise is heard. BLANCHE looks up. Across the river a quartet of young men (RONDINELLA, BIGLER, TADD, and BELL) come running. They're naked, except for TADD, who has his pant legs rolled up and his face buried in a book. BLANCHE watches secretively.*

BIGLER
We're going to be late. Let's go.

BELL
One more!

TADD
He's right. I heard the bells.

RONDINELLA
Ah, he's a fast runner; he'll catch up.

> *RONDINELLA pushes BELL into the river. Laughing, he and BIGLER run off with TADD trailing after. BELL emerges, luxuriating in the water. A graceful slow-motion movement as he bathes in the river. BLANCHE is transfixed.*

> *BELL turns and sees her. BLANCHE gasps and hides behind her sketch pad attempting to be invisible. BELL strains to see who is over there. When BLANCHE looks up and over her pad, he gives a playful wave and runs off. Pause.*

BLANCHE
Well.

> *She looks at the blank sketch pad and quickly attempts to sketch what she saw from memory. Too late, it's gone. She follows.*

GIRL INTERRUPTED
||||||||||||||||||||||||||||||||||||||||||||||||||

> *In the photography compound at the university, MUYBRIDGE stands staring at his pocket watch. He checks the sky. SUSAN, a model, stands awkwardly at the edge of the compound. A bell tolls and the team of assistants suddenly stream onstage to set up the photographic equipment. They are an efficient crew. MUYBRIDGE continues to monitor his watch as well as the activities of the team. A gunshot stops everyone in their tracks.*

RONDINELLA
(*to BIGLER*) Sounds like the veterinary school lost another patient. (*to MUYBRIDGE*) Sir, we now have water running to the tent. The darkroom is fully operational.

[16]

MUYBRIDGE
    Good.

        *MUYBRIDGE approaches SUSAN and manhandles her
        to the track.*

MUYBRIDGE
    Let's get a timing first. It's just two paces. She's a bit shorter so let's
    adjust the level of the rear foreshortening.

        *RONDINELLA runs a tape measure from the ground to the small
        of SUSAN's back.*

RONDINELLA
    Ninety-two centimetres.

MUYBRIDGE
    What's the lens at?

RONDINELLA
    It's at a hundred and five.

MUYBRIDGE
    Let's bring it down to ninety-five. Are you ready with the watch?

BIGLER
    Yep.

MUYBRIDGE
    You're model six.

SUSAN
    I don't know.

MUYBRIDGE
    No, I'm telling you you're model six. She's model six.

SUSAN
    My name's Susan.

TADD
    Model six.

MUYBRIDGE
    Remember that number; we'll call for you by that. Short, medium build,
    about twenty.

TADD
    About twenty.

SUSAN
I'm eighteen.

MUYBRIDGE
Eighteen.

TADD
Got it. Medium build? Not stout?

MUYBRIDGE is checking the sky.

MUYBRIDGE
Uhhhh … no … uh … medium's good enough. We're losing light.
We're losing time. We're losing money! Are the plates ready?

BELL
They're all set.

MUYBRIDGE
Did mail come today, Tadd?

TADD
I'll check.

He runs off.

MUYBRIDGE
Okay, stand by. Let's time this and do it quickly! Ready? Go.

*A rapid-fire clacking noise is heard. SUSAN jumps at the sound
and stands there confused.*

MUYBRIDGE
Go! Oh stop. Reset. What are you waiting for? When I say "Go," you go.
Don't spring the shutters for the timing.

BIGLER
Sorry.

MUYBRIDGE
We don't know what the rate is yet.

BIGLER
I know, sorry.

MUYBRIDGE
Let's go again.

SUSAN
Um …

MUYBRIDGE
Stand by. What?

SUSAN
What would you like?

MUYBRIDGE
What would I like? I'd like you to walk!

SUSAN
Just walk?

MUYBRIDGE
Just walk.

SUSAN
When is the picture taken?

MUYBRIDGE
As you walk.

SUSAN
At what point?

MUYBRIDGE
At all points.

SUSAN
Do you want me to stop along the way?

MUYBRIDGE
No. I just want you to walk.

SUSAN
Okay. Looking where?

MUYBRIDGE
Where you look when you walk. This one is very simple.

SUSAN
(*whispers*) Do I take my clothes off?

MUYBRIDGE
Yes. Not yet. Right now, all we want is to time you walking. Two steps.
It's simple, just walk.

SUSAN
Like this?

> *SUSAN walks. Her gait is awkward and clumsy. TADD returns
> with a bundle of letters.*

MUYBRIDGE

What is that?

SUSAN

What?

MUYBRIDGE

Is that how you walk?

SUSAN

Is it wrong?

MUYBRIDGE

It's pathologically ungraceful. Model six is a normal person, isn't she?

TADD hands MUYBRIDGE the letters, and he starts flipping through them.

TADD

She's supposed to be.

SUSAN

What?

MUYBRIDGE

Just walk again.

SUSAN starts down the track.

MUYBRIDGE

Not so self-consciously. Let your arms swing. No, don't swing them. Just let – wait, why are you doing that with your head? Just be normal. Good God, were you raised by apes?

SUSAN

Huh?

MUYBRIDGE

Where did she come from? A brothel?

TADD

She's one of Eakins's art college models.

MUYBRIDGE

Eakins.

He takes a deep breath and affects as cheery a disposition as he can.

MUYBRIDGE
I'm sorry, just try it again – don't try to "do" anything but walk simply towards the end there. One foot after the other, head up, look out, and just like this –

MUYBRIDGE demonstrates walking.

SUSAN
All right.

MUYBRIDGE
All right.

MUYBRIDGE notices a particular letter and opens it after returning the rest of the stack to TADD.

MUYBRIDGE
Time it.

MUYBRIDGE scans the letter as the men take their positions.

BIGLER
Standing by.

MUYBRIDGE
Go.

He sees something in the letter. The photography compound dissolves.

PORTRAIT OF AN OLDER ORPHAN
||||||||||||||||||||||||||||||||||||||||||||||||||||||||||||||||||||||||||||||

SISTER ANNE-MARIE, a nun from the San Francisco Orphans Asylum appears. Nearby a young man is being photographed. The nun holds an envelope. She presses at the seal, checks the address and postage as she watches the young man. She speaks the contents of the letter to us.

SISTER ANNE-MARIE
Dear Mr. Muybridge, My name is Sister Anne-Marie Lacontre and I serve at the San Francisco Orphans Asylum. I write to you with the knowledge that you are Floredo Muybridge's only living ... relation. This year he will turn fifteen. Now a young man, he is too old to remain at the orphanage. His faith is strong, he is attentive in his prayers, but his spirit is weak and he has little education. I fear for his future as this world preys upon the mild and innocent as he. But he can stay no longer and, without answer from you, we will be forced to turn him to the world upon his next birthday. I write with faith that there is a place for him on God's earth. Enclosed please find a photograph. With blessings to you, Sister Anne-Marie.

The orphanage disappears.

MUYBRIDGE staggers and collapses to his knees.

A group of men, a jury of MUYBRIDGE's peers, enters dressed in topcoats and hats and stands around him in judgment.

The moment is broken as FLORA enters, pregnant. She walks towards MUYBRIDGE. He places his head against her belly; then she helps him to his feet and guides him offstage.

A motion study begins. Several actors form a line, each posed at a different phase of the action of a man collapsing to his knees. They are illuminated sequentially by a quick flash of light that creates a stroboscopic illusion of movement, a Muybridge motion study.

OUTSIDE THE FENCE

BLANCHE comes sneaking in along the fence trying to find a gap or knothole to peek through. Behind the scrim we see what she sees: BELL and RONDINELLA are adjusting the position of a battery of cameras. When BELL leaves her view, she moves to another gap in the fence to keep him in sight. SUSAN enters. As BLANCHE strains to see BELL, who is warming up for a motion study, SUSAN sneaks over and peeks through too.

SUSAN
It gets better.

BLANCHE jumps and pulls back; the view is gone.

SUSAN
Blanche?

BLANCHE
Yes?

SUSAN
It's me. Susan. I modelled for your father.

BLANCHE
Oh. Oh. Oh. Susan.

SUSAN
What are you doing?

BLANCHE
Do you know what's happening here?

SUSAN
Photography.

BLANCHE
Of what?

SUSAN
Animals and people. They need more models, if you're interested.

BLANCHE
What do you do?

SUSAN
You take off your clothes and walk in front of the cameras.

BLANCHE
You can do that?

SUSAN
Well, they're pretty picky about the way you walk.

BLANCHE
But nude?

SUSAN
Sure. What? Just the same as when I'm at the art school.

BLANCHE
But those are paintings. With photographs, it's really you in the end.

SUSAN
Paintbrush or camera, being naked is being naked. Except in this case, I don't get cramps trying to hold still for so long! You could do it.

BLANCHE
I can't imagine.

SUSAN
Trust me. Oh, something's happening now. Can you see?

BLANCHE
Yeah.

SUSAN
Look, that one's practising – see? He's running in front of the cameras.

BLANCHE
Who is he? I've seen him before.

SUSAN
Where?

BLANCHE
Um ... I'm not sure.

SUSAN
He's one of the assistants here; he's pretty sweet and – omigod ...

*The girls pull back from the fence, embarrassed. They look
at each other, look around, and then go back to the gap in
the fence.*

SUSAN
Wow.

BLANCHE
He's completely naked.

SUSAN
Those pants came off like nothing. I guess they're ready to go.

BLANCHE
It's not very private, is it?

SUSAN
Well, that's why they have this fence. So people can't see in.

*BLANCHE shifts her vantage point and then suddenly
screams and pulls away from the fence. SUSAN screams
in response.*

SUSAN
What happened?

BLANCHE whispers.

BLANCHE
I saw an eye.

SUSAN
What?

BLANCHE
An eye in the fence was staring back.

They stare suspiciously at the fence and then try to find a position out of the sightline of whoever might be behind it. They both continue to whisper.

SUSAN

Uh-oh. We should get out of here. I don't want to lose my job for being a pervert.

They start to head out when BELL appears in front of them. He wears trousers but no shirt.

BELL

Hey.

SUSAN

Oh. Ah ... Mr. Balls – Ball.

BELL

Bell.

SUSAN

Bell. That's right, Bell. Mr. Bell.

BELL

Henry.

SUSAN

Susan.

BELL

I remember.

He looks at BLANCHE.

BELL

G'day. (*to SUSAN*) Are you back to model?

SUSAN

Yes.

BELL

And you?

SUSAN

She's considering.

BLANCHE

No, I'm not.

BELL

No? Why are you here?

BLANCHE

What's going on? What are you doing this for?

BELL

Well, for instance, say you're an artist ...

BLANCHE

No, I'm ...

BELL

Well, say you are, and you're going to draw something and you're going to draw this –

He flaps his arm really quickly.

BELL

Or this –

He throws a couple of punches.

BELL

Or this –

He runs, jumps, and kicks.

BELL

Could you draw that?

BLANCHE

I don't know.

BELL

Of course you couldn't. But the cameras can catch everything we can't see.

BLANCHE

Can I watch?

BELL

Well, if you model, you can come in.

BLANCHE

If I can watch, I'll know if I can model.

BELL

Well ... you can't watch. No one watches.

SUSAN
  "Privacy."

BELL
  You'll appreciate that if you choose to model.

BLANCHE
  Don't you watch?

BELL
  No. I work. Everyone there is working. Doing. Not watching.

BLANCHE
  Do you need any extra help?

SUSAN
  Models!

BLANCHE
  If only I knew what that was like.

BELL
  Maybe I can let you see some pictures.

BLANCHE
  Yes, please.

BELL
  "Yes, please." Good. And then I can show you the cameras
  between studies.

BLANCHE
  Yes.

BELL
  Well, come on then.

SUSAN
  I've been practising.

BELL
  Good news.

       *He exits; SUSAN follows. BLANCHE takes another peek through
       the gap in the fence.*

       *MUYBRIDGE appears behind her as though he's in her field of
       vision. Sensing something, he turns and looks. She pulls back
       and exits.*

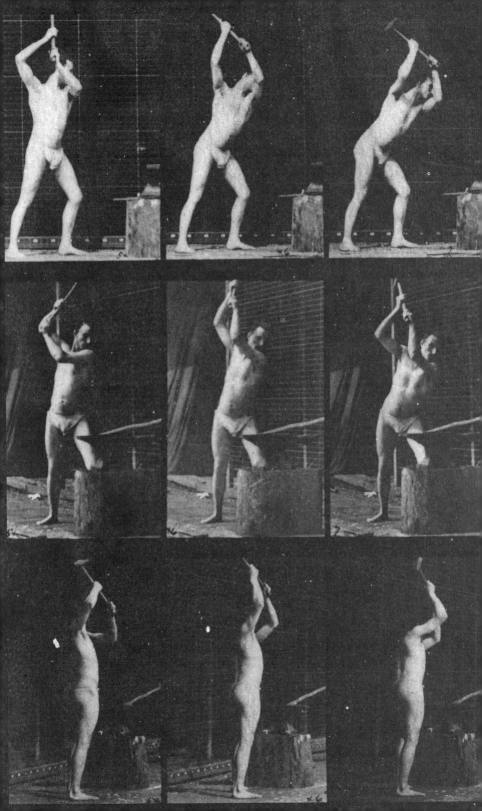

MUYBRIDGE stands in the centre of the compound. He checks his watch. TADD enters with a damp cloth for him. MUYBRIDGE takes it and holds it to his eyes as RONDINELLA and BIGLER enter with an anvil for the next motion study.

MUYBRIDGE

Put it here; I'll mark the spot of the blacksmith. Is your model ready, Mr. Tadd?

TADD

He's changing. I'll check on him.

TADD exits. MUYBRIDGE sinks to the ground with the cloth over his eyes. Eventually he lies on his back with the cloth on his face and directs his assistants from that position. No one seems to regard this as strange.

RONDINELLA

That's good, Bigler. Mark that and give me a focal length.

BIGLER runs a tape measure between the cameras and the anvil.

RONDINELLA

What's the distance?

BIGLER

It looks like it's eleven feet, six and three-quarter inches.

RONDINELLA

Sir, do you want me to switch to the Bigler lenses?

MUYBRIDGE

Bigler?

RONDINELLA

You know, the short ones.

BIGLER

Hey.

MUYBRIDGE

I want the eight-inch lenses.

RONDINELLA

Ah yes, that's what Bigler dreams of too.

BIGLER

Hey!

RONDINELLA exits. BELL enters and scans the compound.

The women enter. They exchange glances upon seeing MUYBRIDGE lying flat-out with a cloth over his face.

MUYBRIDGE

Bell!

BELL walks over and squats beside MUYBRIDGE. As they talk, SUSAN discreetly shows BLANCHE the photography compound. She waves to BIGLER, who nearly drops a lens as he attempts to casually acknowledge her. SUSAN points to the cameras and then heads to the track, where she demonstrates for BLANCHE what it is to move in front of the cameras.

BELL

Sir.

MUYBRIDGE

We need to shoot the pig again.

BELL

Pig?

Offstage RONDINELLA is shouting and clapping.

RONDINELLA

Hey! Stop that! Get out of here!

A pig oinks and grunts.

MUYBRIDGE

Shutter number five didn't fire. We have a missing pig.

BIGLER

Sir, five's working again.

BELL

Aren't we set for the blacksmith?

MUYBRIDGE

Yes, but what about after?

BELL looks at his notes.

BELL
(*winks at SUSAN*) I think it's "woman walking and measuring hip rotation."

MUYBRIDGE
Oh right.

BELL
Maybe we do a pickup tomorrow afternoon.

MUYBRIDGE
How many pigs did we get?

BELL
Um ...

>   *Pages drop from his collection of notes.*

MUYBRIDGE
Quickly.

BELL
I don't know. I'd have to go back and count.

MUYBRIDGE
You need to be better organized.

BELL
I am, but it's a lot of material now and there isn't a lot of structure. Pigs and blacksmiths, performing mule, a woman climbs a ladder. Everything's a little arbitrary.

MUYBRIDGE
We have to go with what's available.

>   *RONDINELLA enters with lenses wrapped in cloth.*

RONDINELLA
Hup!

>   *RONDINELLA tosses a lens to BIGLER, who catches it with a bit of a panic.*

BIGLER
Careful. Geez.

RONDINELLA
Hup!

>   *Another lens.*

RONDINELLA
  Eighty dollars if you drop it!

BIGLER
  Don't do that.

  MUYBRIDGE suddenly springs to his feet and bellows.

MUYBRIDGE
  Where is our model?

  He finds himself face to face with BLANCHE. MUYBRIDGE stares at her with one of his imperceptible yet intimidating expressions. TADD enters.

TADD
  He's on his way. (*motions to SUSAN*) Six, you're next. Get ready. (*points at BLANCHE*) No women.

  SUSAN scampers off. BELL directs BLANCHE towards the darkroom tent; MUYBRIDGE tracks her movement.

BELL
  You can wait in here until after the study.

  She exits into the tent. Thunder rumbles.

RONDINELLA
  That's thunder; we're losing the light.

TADD
  He's here.

  The BLACKSMITH enters sheepishly wearing a loincloth and carrying a hammer.

BLACKSMITH
  Is this necessary?

MUYBRIDGE
  Oh good. Are you ready?

BLACKSMITH
  Why am I wearing this?

MUYBRIDGE
  I believe you said you didn't want to pose nude.

BLACKSMITH
  Nor do I want to wear a diaper.

MUYBRIDGE
    Pelvis cloth.

BLACKSMITH
    I feel like an idiot.

MUYBRIDGE
    It's standard for this.

BLACKSMITH
    Says who?

MUYBRIDGE
    Says me – the photographer that's running this thing. We have to hurry;
    it looks like there's a storm coming.

BLACKSMITH
    Do you know what would happen if I wore a diaper while I worked?

MUYBRIDGE
    We have to see the body.

BLACKSMITH
    Hot metal! I work with hot metal. Not to mention I'd be arrested
    for indecency.

MUYBRIDGE
    But you understand that scientists and artists will use these
    photographs.

BLACKSMITH
    Who exactly is going to see these things?

MUYBRIDGE
    Those who subscribe.

BLACKSMITH
    They have to buy them?

MUYBRIDGE
    Yes.

BLACKSMITH
    How much?

MUYBRIDGE
    One hundred dollars for the series.

BLACKSMITH
    That's good. It rules out any of my mates.

MUYBRIDGE

I assure you – this is for educational purposes – you needn't feel
self-conscious.

BLACKSMITH

Tell ya, though, it gives the wrong idea.

MUYBRIDGE

No, it just helps to see the body without obstruction.

BLACKSMITH

Some idiot artist will paint a scene in a blacksmith's and everyone will
be wearing diapers.

MUYBRIDGE

I doubt it. But they will have an excellent example of form, an exquisite
specimen – if I may – of a strong, masterful blacksmith with excellent
muscle structure and technique. You have a very ... impressive form.

BLACKSMITH

Hmm. Well, let's get on with it.

MUYBRIDGE

Perfect. Just position yourself here and demonstrate a few swings of
the hammer.

> The BLACKSMITH adjusts his loincloth and a potato drops out of
> the front of it. He scrambles to get it, but knocks it away instead.

BLACKSMITH

Oops. Uh. I didn't have anywhere else to keep that. For a bite ... later ...
in case this took a long time. For lunch. You know. Might be all day ...
I didn't know.

MUYBRIDGE

Of course.

BLACKSMITH

Well, um, okay then, let's do this.

MUYBRIDGE

Did you want it back?

BLACKSMITH

What?

MUYBRIDGE

For the picture.

BLACKSMITH
Why? No. It's just for eating. Later.

MUYBRIDGE
The photographs will have significant circulation.

> *Pause. MUYBRIDGE continues to hold the potato extended towards the BLACKSMITH. Complete, simple, sincere non-judgment.*

BLACKSMITH
Right. Okay then. Here quickly.

> *MUYBRIDGE tosses the potato back to the BLACKSMITH, who shoves it down his loincloth.*

BLACKSMITH
How's that?

MUYBRIDGE
A little lower; it looks like a tumour.

> *The BLACKSMITH adjusts it.*

MUYBRIDGE
Nice. Stand by.

RONDINELLA
Clear frame. Electrics?

MUYBRIDGE
And action, Thirty-One / on my mark: three

BIGLER
Go ahead.

MUYBRIDGE
two, one ... mark.

> *The BLACKSMITH swings the hammer while coyly looking towards the camera. A sudden flash accompanied by an absolutely deafening crack of thunder. Everyone jumps or ducks.*

BLACKSMITH
Christ!

> *Pause.*

BIGLER
Whoa.

BELL
   Wow! Who's model thirty-one? Thor?

BLACKSMITH
   Thor just about pooped his diaper, I'll tell you that.

RONDINELLA
   Omigod, look.

TADD
   'Sblood!

BIGLER
   What? What is that?

MUYBRIDGE
   The pig. Lightning hit the pig. No reshoot.

RONDINELLA
   That is absolutely disgusting.

BLACKSMITH
   Am I done? I felt rain.

      Rain.

MUYBRIDGE
   Did we get the sequence?

RONDINELLA
   Yeah. Bigler?

BIGLER
   Uh, yeah, good on my end. How did that happen?

MUYBRIDGE
   Let's get a cover on the equipment. You're done, Thirty-One, thank you.

      *The crew covers up as the BLACKSMITH exits. MUYBRIDGE pulls
      the plates out of the cameras and heads for the darkroom.*

THE ASSISTANT

      *BLANCHE is alone in the darkroom tent. Pictures of a naked
      running man hang to dry from lines stretched across the space.
      She's startled as the tent flap opens and MUYBRIDGE enters with
      the exposed plates from the blacksmith session. He stops short
      when he sees her.*

[36]

MUYBRIDGE
Who are you?

BLANCHE
Blanche?

MUYBRIDGE
Blanche? How did you get in here?

BLANCHE
Mr. Bell ... was ... I was curious, so ... I'm a friend of Susan's.

MUYBRIDGE
Susan?

BLANCHE
A model?

MUYBRIDGE
Six?

BLANCHE
Six?

MUYBRIDGE
Eleven?

BLANCHE
Eleven?

> MUYBRIDGE shows her two sets of images of different women moving.

MUYBRIDGE
(indicating the first) Six. (and then the second) Eleven.

> BLANCHE recognizes her naked friend in one set.

BLANCHE
Oh my. Uh ... Six.

MUYBRIDGE
Are you an Eakins model as well then?

BLANCHE
No, I could never model.

MUYBRIDGE
What do you do?

BLANCHE
  I take care of my father's – I mean I used to take care of the business
  of ... Not to be forward, but I've never seen anything like this and I'm
  very curious and did I hear you were having trouble keeping track of
  the work being done?

MUYBRIDGE
  Well, it's not me who's having difficulty.

BLANCHE
  No of course, but is there perhaps a lack of ...

MUYBRIDGE
  Have you decent penmanship?

BLANCHE
  Yes.

MUYBRIDGE
  Are you comfortable with numbers?

BLANCHE
  Yes.

MUYBRIDGE
  And you don't object to viewing materials such as this or this?

      He flashes the photos of the different women.

BLANCHE
  No.

MUYBRIDGE
  (*points at the naked running man*) Or that?

      *BELL enters. BLANCHE looks from the image to him and then
      quickly finds a neutral piece of ground to look at.*

BLANCHE
  No. I don't object to that.

BELL
  Object to what?

MUYBRIDGE
  Mr. Bell, I want to introduce you to someone.

BELL
  We've met.

MUYBRIDGE

I've hired her to be my assistant, or rather your assistant. She will report to you. She'll catalogue the studies as we go, create some order. Mr. Bell will show you what we need: each series must be identified by the action and the model number; for instance, there is number thirty-three –

BELL

Number thirty-three is me.

MUYBRIDGE

Is this the sort of work you were looking for?

BLANCHE

(*looking at BELL while glancing at the images above*) Yes, it is.

MUYBRIDGE

Mr. Bell, show her the catalogue as it stands. I'll develop this set.

BELL

Happily. Follow me.

> *He exits. BLANCHE heads out, then spins back to speak, but MUYBRIDGE answers ahead of her.*

MUYBRIDGE

The work is piecemeal. A penny a picture catalogued.

BLANCHE

Thank you.

> *She turns to go and spins back again. There is a pause as the two observe each other. A thunderclap breaks the silence. BLANCHE takes this as her cue to get going. MUYBRIDGE stares at her as she exits. Rain pours down.*

THREE SHORT STUDIES OF FLORA

ONE: An Unexpected Downpour

> *Bradley and Rulofson's Gallery, San Francisco, 1872. FLORA, a nineteen-year-old assistant, enters from outdoors. She holds a book over her head in a pathetic attempt at an umbrella.*

FLORA

This is my first San Francisco shower.

MUYBRIDGE
   Is that the Bible?

FLORA
   (*laughs*) No. A collection of plays. I was caught up in the climax –
   a cruel twist of fate. Then it rained.

MUYBRIDGE
   A cruel twist of fate.

FLORA
   And then I saw the Help Wanted sign. Fate again.

MUYBRIDGE
   Ah. Except I'm looking for someone with experience in retouching
   photographs.

   FLORA curtseys coyly.

MUYBRIDGE
   Indeed?

   She nods. He holds out his hand.

MUYBRIDGE
   Eadweard Muybridge. Miss ... Missus ...

   Pause.

FLORA
   Flora.

   She smiles.

MUYBRIDGE
   Miss ... us ...?

FLORA
   Flora.

   The scene shifts.

TWO: Landscapes and Architecture

   *MUYBRIDGE uses tongs to remove a picture from the basin –
   a developing bath. FLORA takes the picture from him and
   examines it. MUYBRIDGE stands behind her.*

FLORA
   Where is this?

MUYBRIDGE
North. Alaska. Or maybe British Columbia. Yes, it's British Columbia.

She raises the photo to her nose.

FLORA
I can smell the air there.

MUYBRIDGE
Those are chemicals.

She smells again.

FLORA
It's so fresh ...

She picks up a second picture.

FLORA
And where's this?

MUYBRIDGE
That? That's just the San Francisco Orphans Asylum. A commissioned photograph. Sad.

FLORA
Don't be. There are far worse places.

She inhales.

And it smells like the north to me.

The scene shifts.

THREE: Cloud Studies

FLORA sneaks up behind MUYBRIDGE and covers his eyes.
He inhales and smiles. She uncovers and looks over his
shoulder. She watches him work for a bit and then comes
around and takes his hand and guides the brush.

FLORA
Lighter. Let go – give your hand over. Lighter, like so. See? Petting the tiniest kitten – pet, pet, pet.

He's overwhelmed by the physical contact. He looks at her.
She lets go of his hand and touches his beard. Then she runs
her fingers through it.

FLORA
So white.

*She runs both hands through his beard, and then runs her fingers
up his temples and into his hair. She starts fluffing out his hair so
that it gets bigger and bigger and wilder and wilder. As she does
this, she starts making whooshing sounds, blowing as if she were
the wind. She speaks in a low, funny voice.*

FLORA
I'm the wind. Whooooo. I'm a giant cloud. Blow, blow, blow.
Blow me away, Mr. Cloud. Blow me away.

He closes his eyes. Blackout. The scream of a horse.

BLANCHE
||||||||||||||||||||||||

Blinding light.

MUYBRIDGE
No!

BLANCHE is there, silhouetted in the doorway of the tent.

BLANCHE
I'm sorry.

MUYBRIDGE
Close the flap!

Darkness.

BLANCHE
I'm sorry.

MUYBRIDGE
Always announce yourself when coming in here. The light will
destroy our work.

BLANCHE
I'm sorry.

MUYBRIDGE
I've covered the plates; you can open the flap.

*Light pours in as BLANCHE enters. She stares at the
hanging photographs.*

BLANCHE

Mr. Bell asked me to come and tell you that they're ready for
the next set.

MUYBRIDGE

It stopped raining?

BLANCHE

Yes, a while ago. You didn't notice? You're like my father,
lost in his work.

MUYBRIDGE

What are we doing?

She shows him her catalogue.

BLANCHE

Woman walking. Does this look right?

MUYBRIDGE

You're fast.

BLANCHE

Can I take this stack away now?

MUYBRIDGE

Yes. (*handing her a stick affixed to a belt*) And here: for the next ·
set the model will wear this around her waist.

BLANCHE

Why? – How about this stack here?

MUYBRIDGE

(*casually demonstrates*) To analyze the movement of her hips – Yes,
take those too – as she walks, the stick swings revealing the precise
angle. Perhaps we'll discover a formula for grace. Though number
six isn't particularly graceful. How do you walk?

BLANCHE

Have her hold a bouquet of flowers and tell her to pretend she's walking
down the aisle to her wedding.

MUYBRIDGE

What would that do?

BLANCHE

It would give her a reason to be graceful. And is this something?

MUYBRIDGE
    What?

BLANCHE
    This boy. It's by itself.

        She shows it to him. He takes it from her and pockets it.

MUYBRIDGE
    No.

BLANCHE
    He has your eyes! Is it you?

MUYBRIDGE
    Me? No, it's not me.

BLANCHE
    Your son?

MUYBRIDGE
    I don't have a son.

BLANCHE
    Oh. Are you married?

MUYBRIDGE
    Once. But ... she's ... she's dead.

BLANCHE
    Oh. I'm sorry –

MUYBRIDGE
    Please tell the men to get ready; I'll be right there.

        He watches as BLANCHE exits.

WEDDING NIGHT
IIIIIIIIIIIIIIIIIIIIIIIIIIIIIIIIIIIIIIIIIIIIIIII

        *Bells ring. FLORA enters. MUYBRIDGE lifts her and carries her
        in his arms across the threshold and into a bedroom on their
        wedding night. He sets her down and gazes at her for a moment.
        There's an awkward pause.*

MUYBRIDGE
    Well ...

FLORA
    Well ...

MUYBRIDGE
Well, I guess you've done this before.

   Beat.

FLORA
I didn't love my first husband, you know? Does it count if there's
no love? Am I a bad person to leave? My father was ... well ...
anyway ... I had to get away. There was a chance and I took it.
I had to do it. I would have died.

   Beat.

But I didn't love my first husband – I thought I did – but I didn't. I didn't
know how love could really feel, until I felt it now. Am I a bad person?

MUYBRIDGE
No.

   *He kisses her gently. She steps back and reaches to undo her dress,
   then stops. MUYBRIDGE covers his eyes. Blackout.*

   *From out of the darkness a motion study begins. In a flickering
   light, two women slowly remove their gowns as they walk upstage.*

OBSCENITY
||||||||||||||||||||||||||||||||

   *In DR. PEPPER's office, MRS. HARRISON holds a charcoal sketch
   of a nude man's pelvis. PEPPER shakes his head as he looks at it.
   EAKINS sits quite far away with his back to them, looking like a
   punished schoolboy.*

PEPPER
Well, he's fired. Simple. I'll write the dismissal notice right now.

MRS. HARRISON
In a class for girls! He simply tore the cloth away from the male
model, revealing ...

PEPPER
There's no excuse.

MRS. HARRISON
My niece was traumatized. This is not what I expect when I donate
so generously to the university.

PEPPER
Indeed.

[45]

EAKINS

It's anatomy. Life drawing. The student was struggling to connect the leg to the torso. I tried to explain what was wrong, but then I thought, just look for yourself how it works.

MRS. HARRISON

A young lady needs only know that a man's leg does eventually connect to his torso. But the juncture is hardly worthy of artistic representation.

PEPPER

Of course. Here it is then. Dismissed.

He hands EAKINS the letter.

EAKINS

Very well. Then let me say: Puritans! How is this different than Muybridge? Because the students were women? Must women be kept from reality?

MRS. HARRISON

Who's Muybridge?

PEPPER

No one. Never heard of him. Who? Muybridge? Oh him. Unrelated events. Scientist. Nothing / like this. There aren't any

EAKINS

He's a genius. And he's revealing the mystery of motion. And nobody questions the necessity of fully nude models in his case.

PEPPER

girls. Or students. Girl students. It's not a class. It's photography. It's research. For science.

MRS. HARRISON

Fully?

EAKINS

Nude.

PEPPER

Well, I suppose a horse is technically always nude if that's what you want to call it.

MRS. HARRISON

And nobody questions it?

EAKINS
    Nobody.

    The scene shifts.

    A motion study begins. A line of men violently swing a pickaxe.
    They freeze, creating an image in sequence, each posed at a
    different phase of the action.

FLORA'S SCRAPBOOK
||||||||||||||||||||||||||||||||||||||||||||||||||||||||

    A night in. Clocks ticking. FLORA lies on the floor looking at her
    scrapbook and sorting images. MUYBRIDGE watches her intently.

MUYBRIDGE
    What do you think of the name "Floredo"?

FLORA
    Who's that?

MUYBRIDGE
    If we ever had a son.

FLORA
    A son?

MUYBRIDGE
    Floredo, after you.

FLORA
    That's sweet.

MUYBRIDGE
    Floredo Helios. "Helios," after my work.

FLORA
    You'd name a baby after work?

MUYBRIDGE
    Yes? Why? My creations? My art. It's not like I'm a quarryman and I'm
    suggesting we name him "Stone."

FLORA
    That was my first husband's name.

MUYBRIDGE
    Bad example.

    Beat.

MUYBRIDGE
Do you want a baby?

FLORA
A baby?

MUYBRIDGE
Yes.

FLORA
I suppose.

MUYBRIDGE
You suppose?

FLORA
Can we go to the theatre?

MUYBRIDGE
The theatre?

FLORA
We never go out.

MUYBRIDGE
But the theatre?

FLORA
What's wrong with the theatre?

MUYBRIDGE
I get bored easily.

FLORA
I get bored easily.

MUYBRIDGE
You need something to fill your time.

FLORA
That's what I'm asking you for.

MUYBRIDGE
Something with meaning.

FLORA
That's what I'm asking you for.

The clock ticks. Blackout.

> *MUYBRIDGE is strapping an apparatus to the waist of SUSAN,
> who is naked. The apparatus consists mainly of a belt and a long
> straight stick that runs upward along the length of the spine
> clearing the top of the woman's head. The device, which moves
> back and forth like the arm of a metronome, is an attempt to
> measure the motion and angle of the hips as she walks.*

MUYBRIDGE
(*a quick tug on the strap*) Is that too tight, Six?

SUSAN
Ha, you've never worn a corset.

MUYBRIDGE
Are we ready?

TEAM
Ready.

MUYBRIDGE
Good. Miss, please record.

> *He points at the assembled team, one by one. BLANCHE scribbles
> what they say.*

SUSAN
Model six.

BIGLER
Chronograph set to one thirty-seven.

BELL
Eight lateral, eight rear at ninety degrees.

RONDINELLA
Walking, measuring hip rotation.

TADD
Costume: nude.

MUYBRIDGE
Ready?

RONDINELLA
Just start back a little farther, Miss.

> *SUSAN walks to the starting point.*

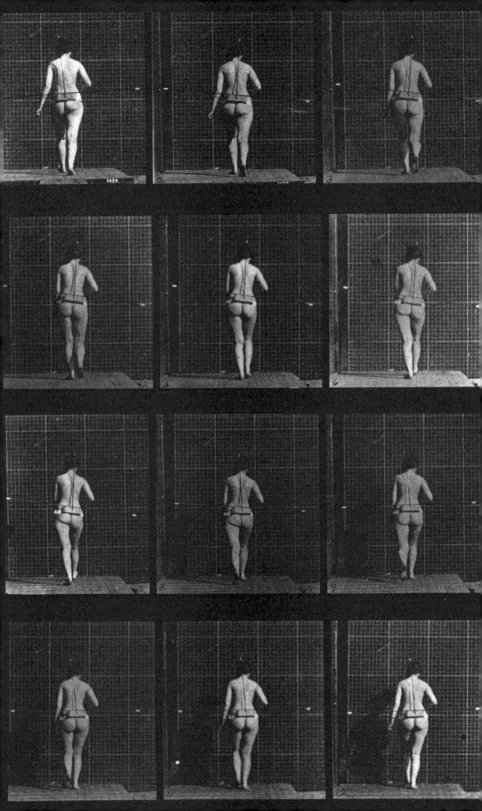

MUYBRIDGE
  That's good there. Standing by. On my mark.

RONDINELLA
  Clear frame. Electrics.

BIGLER
  Go ahead.

MUYBRIDGE
  Three, two, one ... mark.

  The photography compound dissolves.

METRONOME
IIIIIIIIIIIIIIIIIIIIIIIIIIIIIIIIIIIIII

  *Music. As SUSAN begins her walk, the scene shifts and the stage
  transforms into shimmering light as the grid intensifies. Three
  other women walk onstage, each with a device like the one above.
  They begin to move in sync – walking forward and back on the
  stage. The swinging needle attached to their hips becomes a
  metronome.*

  *Five men walk onstage – following the rhythm set by the women's
  walk. There is a surreal dance underscored by the ticking of a
  clock. MUYBRIDGE, intently observing the shapes and patterns
  of the bodies, drifts through the choreography. One by one,
  figures exit, leaving MUYBRIDGE alone with the sound of the
  ticking clock.*

IMPOSSIBLE COUPLE
IIIIIIIIIIIIIIIIIIIIIIIIIIIIIIIIIIIIIIIIIIIIIIIIIIII

  FLORA enters.

FLORA
  She's so lovely. You'll see. You'll make me jealous, that's how lovely
  she is. I'll just shrivel up / and waste

MUYBRIDGE
  Shhh shh shh.

FLORA
  away; I'll be reduced to a wisp, a vapour.

MUYBRIDGE
  The carriage is waiting.

FLORA
Is that what you're wearing?

She fishes something out of his beard, inspects it.

MUYBRIDGE
Why? What's wrong with it?

FLORA
I think that's carrot.

MUYBRIDGE
We'll be in the dark anyway.

FLORA
We had carrots Tuesday.

MUYBRIDGE
Do you want me to change?

FLORA
Let's see.

She spins him towards a mirror and looks at their reflection standing side by side. She, dressed elegantly and elaborately. He, dressed like Muybridge.

FLORA
No, it's perfect. Dramatic. Unlikely. Impossible.

A kiss. And they're gone.

THE GHOSTWRITER
||||||||||||||||||||||||||||||||||||||||||||||||||

Henry LARKYNS is watching a play through a set of opera glasses. A man, COPPINGER, enters and sits beside him holding a notepad.

COPPINGER
How do you want to review this play?

LARKYNS
What did I hire you for?

COPPINGER
To write your review for you.

Beat.

COPPINGER
I just don't want to misrepresent your point of view.

[52]

LARKYNS
Then write it a dozen different ways and I'll choose the one that suits
me. There's a girl there.

He hands COPPINGER the opera glasses.

COPPINGER
Where?

LARKYNS
In the opposite box. I think she's with her father – the dumpy guy with
all the hair.

COPPINGER
In the red?

LARKYNS
That's her.

COPPINGER
Right.

LARKYNS
What do you know about her?

COPPINGER
I know that's not her father.

LARKYNS
Grandfather?

COPPINGER
Husband.

LARKYNS
Give me those. (*looking at her again*) Cradle-robber.

COPPINGER
I think she's a divorcee.

LARKYNS
What about him? Perhaps a gold miner?

COPPINGER
He's a landscape photographer. Calls himself "Helios, the
Flying Camera."

LARKYNS
Never heard of him.

COPPINGER

You haven't seen his photographs of clouds? They're devastatingly brilliant.

LARKYNS

Helios. I think I'll introduce myself after the show.

>   *Pause.*

COPPINGER

Can I watch the rest from here?

LARKYNS

No. "Ghost" in the term "ghostwriter" refers to the invisible nature of the role ... so go rattle your chains down in general admission.

>   *COPPINGER skulks out. LARKYNS turns to look for FLORA again.*

LARKYNS

Now where did you go, my vision of loveliness?

>   *He looks back and MUYBRIDGE is in his field of vision staring back. They stare in each other's direction until, unsettled, LARKYNS puts down his glasses.*

LARKYNS

Gawkers. Everywhere.

>   *He exits. MUYBRIDGE continues to stare. Lights fade.*

AN INVITATION TO THE THEATRE
IIIIIIIIIIIIIIIIIIIIIIIIIIIIIIIIIIIIIIIIIIIIIIIIIIIIIIIIIIIIIIIIIIIIIIIIIIIIII

>   *In the lobby moments later. FLORA is surveying the crowd and MUYBRIDGE is looking at the program.*

MUYBRIDGE

No one is credited with the scenic painting – obviously the man has some sense of shame.

>   *LARKYNS descends upon them.*

LARKYNS

Helios, the Flying Camera!

MUYBRIDGE

Sir?

LARKYNS
Larkyns, Henry Larkyns. Sorry for intruding. Just had to introduce myself. I've seen your work.

MUYBRIDGE
Yes?

LARKYNS
Fantastic. (*to FLORA*) Good evening.

MUYBRIDGE
Oh yes ... uh ... my wife. Mrs. Muybridge.

LARKYNS
A pleasure, Mrs. Muybridge.

> *He kisses her hand.*

FLORA
Oh, call me Flora.

LARKYNS
I wouldn't dream of it.

COPPINGER
Psst.

LARKYNS
Excuse me.

> *LARKYNS turns away to pay off COPPINGER and receive his review.*

FLORA
I know you.

LARKYNS
Oh, do you?

MUYBRIDGE
How?

FLORA
You're the theatre critic for the *Post*.

LARKYNS
Yes, one of my passions. The other is art. Say, you're an expert. Do you think I could pick your brain about a few art-related questions. I'm writing a feature about the pursuit of beauty in contemporary painting.

MUYBRIDGE
The *Post*, eh?

LARKYNS
I'm always pitching stories about local artists. Perhaps I could come by your place sometime to talk.

MUYBRIDGE
Perhaps.

LARKYNS
Tomorrow?

MUYBRIDGE
Uh –

LARKYNS
Perfect; and much appreciated. As a gesture of gratitude, I have for you some tickets to Thursday's performance of *The Murderous Cuckold*.

FLORA
Oh, I want to see that!

LARKYNS
I know the title makes it sound salacious, but let me tell you, it really is! I have to review it ... so ... I need to see it again and this time bring a notepad.

> He chuckles. FLORA chuckles. LARKYNS chuckles again. FLORA chuckles again. MUYBRIDGE clears his throat.

MUYBRIDGE
Unfortunately I have many engagements Thursday.

FLORA
You're always busy.

MUYBRIDGE
The answer is no.

FLORA
You never take me to the theatre.

MUYBRIDGE
We're at the theatre right now.

FLORA
First time in ages.

MUYBRIDGE

And a waste of money.

FLORA

Well, these tickets are free.

MUYBRIDGE

And I said I'm busy.

FLORA

Well, I'll go by myself.

MUYBRIDGE

You will not.

LARKYNS

No, indeed that wouldn't be right. Though, I suppose … I could escort
her to the theatre and home safely.

FLORA

Oh, could he?

MUYBRIDGE

I don't want you to trouble yourself.

LARKYNS

Well, I have to go anyway. And a woman alone at the theatre – tsk-tsk.
I know, as a man, I'd feel uncomfortable with it.

FLORA

Please.

MUYBRIDGE

All right. You see, Flora is, by no little degree, more interested in the
theatre than I am.

LARKYNS

It's often the case.

FLORA

I have to plead.

MUYBRIDGE

It's all so artificial. And the stories are always the same: a damsel,
a villain, his comeuppance.

LARKYNS

Well, people like a good comeuppance.

FLORA

I like a good comeuppance.

MUYBRIDGE

Yes, but what does it really mean?

LARKYNS

Just a temporary distraction from your troubles.

> LARKYNS and FLORA smile at each other as she takes the tickets.
> MUYBRIDGE watches them as the theatre lobby dissolves.

MODEL NINETY-FIVE
||||||||||||||||||||||||||||||||||||||||||||||||||||||||

> BELL and TADD are practising a leapfrog. They each wear
> loincloths. TADD stands midway down the track, crouched over,
> and BELL is about to take a running jump.

BELL

Ready?

TADD

You have to jump high.

BELL

Don't worry. Don't raise your head as I'm going over.

> BELL starts down the track. TADD straightens, forcing BELL
> to abort the attempt.

TADD

My gosh. Why would I?

BELL

Tadd!

TADD

Sorry, I didn't know you were going.

BELL

I'm going. Keep tucked. I don't want to catch anything on the way over.

> He starts again as SUSAN enters wearing a model's gown
> and carrying a newspaper. TADD straightens. BELL stumbles
> to a stop.

BELL

Tadd!

TADD

(*to SUSAN*) I don't think you're supposed to be here. During the male studies –

SUSAN

There are chickens in the waiting area. Chickens.

TADD

Still, the rules –

SUSAN

I won't look. Unless you don't mind. I wouldn't mind if I were you.

TADD

No, it's fine. (*to BELL*) Do you want to switch?

BELL

Just keep tucked.

TADD

And *you* keep tucked.

BELL

Let's just get this one.

> *BELL psyches himself up for the jump. MUYBRIDGE enters followed by BLANCHE, who shields her eyes with her notebook.*

> *SUSAN, in a model's gown, lies on her side away from the action, reading a newspaper.*

RONDINELLA

We're clear.

BELL

Okay.

MUYBRIDGE

On your time.

BIGLER

Standing by.

> *He runs. MRS. HARRISON enters and, seeing her, TADD straightens up again and BELL collides with him. They scramble behind some cameras to hide themselves.*

> *PEPPER runs in.*

PEPPER

Muybridge! Visitor alert! Everybody dressed! She's headed this –
(*seeing MRS. HARRISON*) Oh good, you found it.

MUYBRIDGE

What's going on?

PEPPER

Ah, Mrs. Harrison, Eadweard Muybridge, photographer.

*MRS. HARRISON looks between the seminaked men, SUSAN in
her diaphanous gown lounging on the ground, and MUYBRIDGE.*

MRS. HARRISON

So you're responsible for this depravity?

MUYBRIDGE

Depravity?

She flashes a photograph at MUYBRIDGE. He tenses.

MRS. HARRISON

I suppose science has much to learn from the wiggle of a naked
girl's buttocks?

MUYBRIDGE

Listen: I strip the clothes away not to see the flesh, but to better see the
motion. If I were able, I'd strip away the flesh as well in order to see
the muscle, then strip the muscle to see the bone, and I'd even throw
away the very skeleton if it could afford me the opportunity to see the
unencumbered essence of an action. That is what interests me.

MRS. HARRISON

But what interests your subscribers? And how much will you pander
to their baser instincts in order to sell your photographs?

MUYBRIDGE

A vast and comprehensive study conducted with a rigorous
methodology will sell the work.

MRS. HARRISON

Says the man safely behind the camera.

MUYBRIDGE

Why don't you watch us work, then, and see for yourself? Gentlemen,
prepare for another study.

MUYBRIDGE heads to the track.

RONDINELLA
What's the subject?

MUYBRIDGE
Man, walking.

TADD
Model?

MUYBRIDGE
(*to BLANCHE*) Miss, please record. This will be model ninety-five.
An ex-athlete, age, about sixty.

MUYBRIDGE starts to undress.

MRS. HARRISON
What are you doing?

MUYBRIDGE
In front of the cameras there is only the action. Each subject is simply
another animal in the bestiary.

MRS. HARRISON
Dr. Pepper!

PEPPER
Muybridge!

MRS. HARRISON
This is un–

*She stops, shocked, transfixed as are the other members of the
compound. MUYBRIDGE is naked. Music plays – a variation of
the music heard in the prologue.*

MUYBRIDGE
Rondinella!

RONDINELLA
Clear frame.

TADD
Clear.

RONDINELLA
Electrics?

BIGLER
Go ahead.

RONDINELLA
   Action, on my mark. Three, two, one ... mark.

> *Music swells and takes over the space. As he walks, he leaves behind a trail of images: frame by frame of his walk. Then MUYBRIDGE is gone, replaced only by the series of images. The music reaches a climax. A gunshot. Blackout.*
>
> *Projection (image): Face of Eadweard Muybridge*
>
> *Muybridge's face returns to stare out at the house.*

END OF ACT ONE

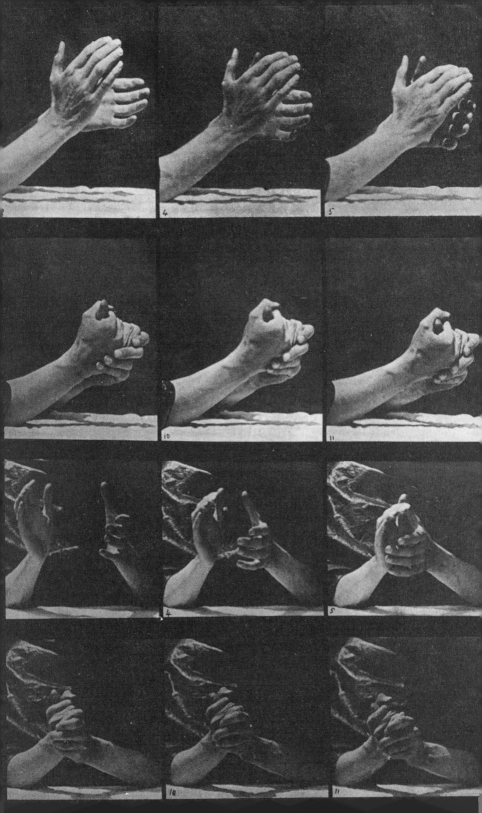

ACT TWO
The Persistence of Vision

MELODRAMA
||||||||||||||||||||||||||||||||||||||||

> *Applause. The front curtain lifts, revealing FLORA and LARKYNS*
> *backstage at the theatre. The leading ACTRESS, wearing her*
> *dressing gown, is giving them a tour of the venue. They walk*
> *onto the set.*

ACTRESS
And this is the stage.

FLORA
Wow, look at all the seats!

LARKYNS
That's a lot of eyes on you.

FLORA
Oh, I couldn't imagine. I really don't like being watched.

LARKYNS
I find that hard to believe.

FLORA
No, it's true. At home I'm constantly being stared at.

ACTRESS
Like you're a child? About to do something wrong?

FLORA
Yes!

ACTRESS
This is different.

FLORA
How?

ACTRESS

Because here when you do something you shouldn't, nobody disapproves.

FLORA

Why not?

ACTRESS

Silly girl. Because it makes the story better!

LARKYNS

Let's pretend we're actors!

FLORA

Yes!

ACTRESS

Yes!

LARKYNS

Teach us one of the scenes.

ACTRESS

Certainly. Why don't we skip to the climax? You be me.

FLORA

All right.

ACTRESS

Put on this tiara.

FLORA

It's glamorous!

ACTRESS

Henry, you're the rogue.

LARKYNS

Got it.

ACTRESS

Oh, it'll be a stretch for sure, but I'll guide you. And I'll play the murderer at the end too.

She produces a pistol.

FLORA

Is that real?

ACTRESS
It will be in a minute.

LARKYNS
Where do we stand?

ACTRESS
In the light!

A spotlight appears. She instructs LARKYNS.

ACTRESS
You're waiting for your lover, who has agreed to meet you in the garden. But it's so dark that she can only feel her way through the night. (*to FLORA*) Close your eyes, sweetie. Feel for your lover.

FLORA holds out her hands and starts feeling for LARKYNS. The ACTRESS helps guide her hands to his.

ACTRESS
Now you say, "Is that you, my love?"

FLORA
Is that you, my love?

ACTRESS
And you say, "We must steal away before we are discovered."

FLORA
We –

ACTRESS
Not you, him.

FLORA
Sorry.

LARKYNS
We must steal away before we are discovered.

ACTRESS
And you say, "Kiss me once before we go."

FLORA
Kiss me once before ...

ACTRESS
And then the lovers kiss. Well, let's see it!

FLORA

I don't suppose I should do that part.

ACTRESS

Oh come on. It's acting. It doesn't count.

LARKYNS

It's just make-believe.

FLORA

Just make-believe.

LARKYNS

Just acting.

FLORA

Just acting.

> *They kiss. Long and passionately. The ACTRESS pulls*
> *a gun on them.*

ACTRESS

And now enters the rogue's jilted lover. "Luciano" – that's your name –
"I thought I was the only one. Who is this troll?"

FLORA

You're so good.

LARKYNS

I love this part. And I've always wanted a dramatic death scene.

> *FLORA claps excitedly.*

FLORA

Do I get to die too?

ACTRESS

Yes, but offstage.

FLORA

Oh – that's disappointing.

ACTRESS

Isn't it though?

> *She takes aim and a gunshot rings out as the lights snap to black.*

      MUYBRIDGE stands in the darkroom examining a gun.
      A voice emerges from the darkness.

SISTER ANNE-MARIE
    You are Floredo Muybridge's only living ... relation. I fear for
    his future as this world preys upon the mild and innocent as he.
    I write with faith that there is a place for him on God's earth.
    Enclosed please find a photograph.

BLANCHE
    (*offstage*) Clear to enter?

MUYBRIDGE
    No!

      He hides the gun.

MUYBRIDGE
    Yes. Come in.

      BLANCHE enters and light fills the space. Images of MUYBRIDGE's
      walk hang drying from the line. BLANCHE stops short when she sees
      them, looks away, but then occasionally glances back in fascination
      whenever she detects MUYBRIDGE isn't looking at her. She holds a
      stack of images and the catalogue.

BLANCHE
    You really surprised everyone. These are recorded.

MUYBRIDGE
    What do women do?

BLANCHE
    Pardon?

MUYBRIDGE
    There should be more to this than these obvious poses: walking,
    running, hammering, throwing. What about the more delicate
    and ephemeral and feminine, like dancing and uh ... or ... right?
    What more do women do?

BLANCHE
    Well, I suppose poor women do chores. And rich women have
    to work ... at being fancy.

      She mimes flirting with a fan.

MUYBRIDGE

Yes, yes, yes! Those. Delicate gestures and perhaps personalized
moments of ... Can you write in some suggestions that I can
request of the models, or, and, if you would like to –

BLANCHE

Oh, and children! Women raise children. Would you want to have
some children doing –

MUYBRIDGE

No.

> RONDINELLA, BELL, and BIGLER pop their heads into the tent.

BELL

Lunch break!

RONDINELLA

We're going down to the river to eat.

BIGLER

And ... and talk!

BELL

In nature.

RONDINELLA

And be infuriatingly profound. Are you coming?

BELL

Beautiful view down there!

BLANCHE

Oh ...

RONDINELLA

Come on!

BLANCHE

I have to stay and ...

BELL

Last chance to see the river!

BLANCHE

Really? Why?

BELL

All new water tomorrow.

BLANCHE
  I ... (*looking to MUYBRIDGE*) suppose.

BELL
  Wizard!

  *They run off. MUYBRIDGE is staring at her. She becomes
  self-conscious.*

  *BLANCHE nods, picks up her catalogue, and is about to exit
  when she looks at the photos on the line.*

BLANCHE
  Do you think this is how the world really is? A series of little moments
  disconnected from one other like grains of sand.

MUYBRIDGE
  I think, perhaps, yes.

BLANCHE
  Yes? No. Can't be, can it?

  *MUYBRIDGE thinks, then goes to unpack his zoöpraxiscope as
  BLANCHE gestures to some images of a woman climbing steps.*

BLANCHE
  Because then is she a different person than she is? Does one person
  end when the other begins?

MUYBRIDGE
  Perhaps.

BLANCHE
  No, it can't be like that. Because a person can remember themselves
  in earlier times.

MUYBRIDGE
  Or is memory just a trick of the mind?

BLANCHE
  What's that?

MUYBRIDGE
  I call it a zoöpraxiscope. A "life viewer."

BELL
  (*offstage*) Miss, we're going!

BLANCHE
  I'll catch up!

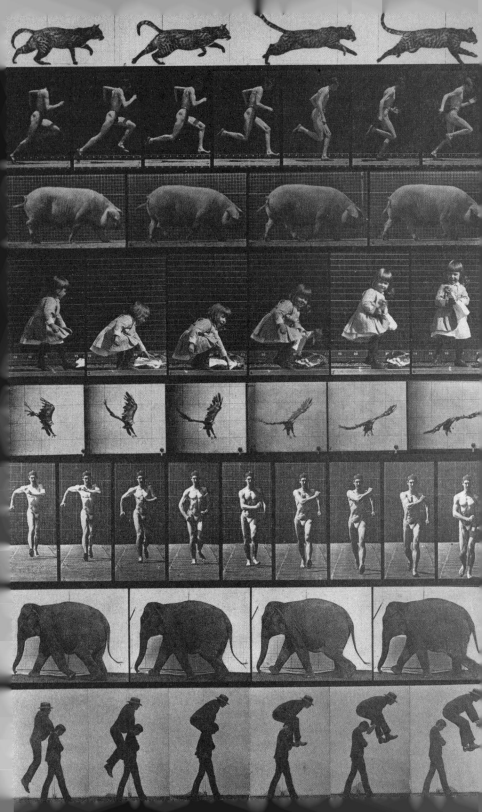

MUYBRIDGE
 Watch.

>*He turns the crank and a still image comes to life. We see a series
of animated Muybridge images: animals walking; people moving,
climbing, lifting, dancing. BLANCHE gasps.*

BLANCHE
 It's alive!

MUYBRIDGE
 Run for your life, little piggie!

BLANCHE
 Oh! It's like a memory.

MUYBRIDGE
 Isn't it?

BLANCHE
 Which anyone can see.

MUYBRIDGE
 And we can stop it for a moment –

>*He freezes the image.*

 Investigate, contemplate, and then –

>*He spins the wheel and the image animates.*

BLANCHE
 Continue. Oh!

>*BLANCHE is mesmerized. She touches him.
MUYBRIDGE notes the contact.*

MUYBRIDGE
 Oh, and here's uh ... number six.

>*Projection (image): Susan, model six*

>*The projection shows images of SUSAN from the earlier motion
study with the metronome-like device attached to her hips*

MUYBRIDGE
 You see, this is wonderful. Very symmetrical, very nice carriage.
 I like this – I like this very much; may I tell you why?

BLANCHE
 Of course.

>*As he talks, the image slows, stops, moves again. Eventually it
grows in size and takes over the space.*

MUYBRIDGE

First, looking directly from behind, we have the notion of symmetry.
This is the world of pairs: dichotomies. Doubles. Dark and light. Good
and evil. Hate and love. Second, as the stick sways like a metronome
counting out time, we have the notion of the clock – notice, its motor
is the woman's hips – this is the next key to humanity; for it is the
world of the circle. It's the circulation of the blood, the pounding of the
heart, birth, death, rebirth ... eternity. And finally against the backdrop
of the grid we have the third aspect of humanity: the line. Beginning,
middle, and end. The cause and the effect. It is our history, our logic,
our science – the way we can understand the symmetry and the circle.
So there it is – all in one study. Symmetry, pairs, dichotomies; circles,
cycles, rhythm; lines, logic, and reason. From this we construct reality.

*MUYBRIDGE watches BLANCHE watch the images. The scene
shifts as the projected images are replaced by live bodies.*

MUYBRIDGE LOOKS

*MUYBRIDGE obsessively observes a world of motion around
him – repetitive gestures and actions that are broken into
components.*

*As MUYBRIDGE tracks the action, BLANCHE observes him,
recording details of the studies in the catalogue.*

*A group of men each put on a jacket with a flourish. A man
walks with a package and a walking stick. A man walks with
an umbrella, opening it and checking the sky. A woman pushes
another woman. Two women sweep. A man climbs over a chair
as performed by four bodies. A woman throws up into a bucket.
A man shovels. A man puts on his bowler hat with a flair. A man
opens a book and registers surprise. A man climbs a set of stairs.*

The world of motion comes to a sudden halt.

TECHNICAL DIFFICULTIES

*The team, a bit exhausted by the pace, is setting up for yet another
motion study.*

TADD

Next.

SUSAN enters in a model's gown and carrying a hat. BLANCHE follows. TADD escorts EAKINS into the photography compound and shows him around. TADD gives a little wave to MUYBRIDGE, who ignores his presence.

Throughout the scene BELL distracts BLANCHE by playfully positioning himself in her personal space as he works.

SUSAN
I want to try this trick with a hat for the sequence. Do you think I should?

BLANCHE
Oh yes!

MUYBRIDGE
Are we standing by?

EAKINS
Looking good, Susan!

SUSAN waves.

MUYBRIDGE
I said, are we standing by?

SUSAN
Oh, ready.

SUSAN takes off her gown and holds it out for BLANCHE.

EAKINS
Muybridge.

MUYBRIDGE
Eakins.

EAKINS
I'll station myself here. Let me know if I can be of assistance.

SUSAN
Psst! Blanche.

BLANCHE takes the gown.

RONDINELLA
Almost ready.

MUYBRIDGE
On my mark.

RONDINELLA
   Oops. What the – wait!

   BLANCHE places the gown back over SUSAN's shoulders.

MUYBRIDGE
   Bigler?

BIGLER
   What? I've dialled it back to three-seventy. Isn't that what you want?

EAKINS
   Ed, did you see this one I did?

   EAKINS has strolled over and shows MUYBRIDGE a print.
   Tadd has followed.

MUYBRIDGE
   Hmm.

EAKINS
   Quite nice isn't it?

TADD
   That's gorgeous.

BIGLER
   Sir?

EAKINS
   I call it "History of a Jump."

TADD
   I get it.

MUYBRIDGE
   What's your action, Model Six?

SUSAN
   I'm going to kick my hat and make it land on my head.

MUYBRIDGE
   You can do that?

SUSAN
   Yes. It's whimsical.

MUYBRIDGE
   Wonderful. Open it to around one forty-five, Bigler.

BIGLER
   All right, give me a second.

EAKINS

"History of a Jump" – sums it up doesn't it?

MUYBRIDGE

Yes, yes. It's quite clear.

EAKINS

You see, all the poses are on one plate. You see everything at once. Not like this system, where it's individual isolated images.

MUYBRIDGE

Well –

EAKINS

I used a Marey Wheel. I call it the photographic gun. (*points his finger at MUYBRIDGE*) Pow. You just follow your subject with it like you would with a gun and spin the wheel at the desired rate and all the parts of the action are recorded on one plate.

MUYBRIDGE

We're ready to go.

> *SUSAN removes her gown again, handing it to BLANCHE.*

EAKINS

It's very versatile and portable.

MUYBRIDGE

My system is very accurate and consistent and dependable.

TADD

I showed him the new foreshortening rig.

MUYBRIDGE

Are we standing by?

BIGLER

Go ahead.

MUYBRIDGE

On my mark. Three / two –

RONDINELLA

Hold.

> *SUSAN gets dressed again.*

MUYBRIDGE

What?

EAKINS
  I just think this is more sensual. It makes my heart ache.

TADD
  Mmm ...

MUYBRIDGE
  What's going on?

RONDINELLA
  We got light in the trap. These plates are contaminated.

MUYBRIDGE
  Bell!

TADD
  (*to EAKINS*) This never happens.

>   *BELL enters.*

MUYBRIDGE
  We need a reload to the lateral three.

BELL
  Not again.

>   *BELL exits.*

TADD
  Or rarely, rather.

MUYBRIDGE
  What's the range of motion, Six?

SUSAN
  Just like this.

>   *She shows with a sort of short hand gesture what she intends*
>   *to do without doing it.*

EAKINS
  With the photographic gun you just load it once, lock it up, and –
  boom – like that, you're ready. I can knock off a series start to finish
  in under a minute. Great for a natural environment.

TADD
  It sounds good.

>   *BELL enters with a fresh plate and tries to load the cameras.*

MUYBRIDGE
　Do you need to practise it?

SUSAN
　I don't want to use up my good ones without the cameras ready.

MUYBRIDGE
　All right, let's go now please!

　　　SUSAN disrobes and waits.

MUYBRIDGE
　Standing by.

BIGLER
　Go ahead.

MUYBRIDGE
　On my mark.

BELL
　No, no, no, no! Not yet!

RONDINELLA
　We're *not* standing by!

　　　SUSAN puts her gown back on and walks over to MUYBRIDGE.

SUSAN
　(*to MUYBRIDGE*) If you think it'll be a little longer, might I get
　some tea to warm up?

MUYBRIDGE
　No, we're ready to go.

SUSAN
　I've never had goose pimples in so many places.

　　　She laughs apologetically.

MUYBRIDGE
　Just stay put, can't waste time with models running off. What's
　happening?

RONDINELLA
　The latch is stuck – the plate's not sitting right.

BELL
　Son of a –

MUYBRIDGE

    Get out of the way!

      He starts manhandling the box containing the glass plate.
      Everyone crowds in.

EAKINS

    Makes you wonder if there's a better system.

      TADD laughs ingratiatingly.

MUYBRIDGE

    This never happens.

SUSAN

    Should I get tea now?

MUYBRIDGE

    No.

EAKINS

    Is it backwards?

MUYBRIDGE

    No, I think I know how it goes being the fucking inventor!

      MUYBRIDGE loses it. He tears the plate from the camera, lifts it high
      above his head, and starts to throw it down at SUSAN's feet. Blackout.
      The sound of glass shattering.

BRAINSTORM
||||||||||||||||||||||||||||||||||||

      In the photography compound, a very tense mood. BLANCHE
      slowly bandages SUSAN's eye. The rest are gathered around
      them at a distance from MUYBRIDGE, watching.

MUYBRIDGE

    In every animal there is one consistent and steady action. A
    muscle which acts before all others, a muscle corralled in bone,
    and blood, and skin, encased in darkness. That lifelong rhythm,
    that constant straining that connects us all, yet hidden inside
    us never to be seen. Wouldn't that be something to witness?
    To capture. To study. Thump-thump. Rondinella?

RONDINELLA

    Sir?

MUYBRIDGE
Could you find me such a subject?

RONDINELLA
Are you suggesting ...?

MUYBRIDGE
I am.

RONDINELLA
But what ... Where would we get ... How would we reveal ...
to photograph ... You see what I'm saying?

MUYBRIDGE
I'll leave that up to you.

RONDINELLA
Sir.

   He exits.

MUYBRIDGE
Now. The work must continue.

TADD
I may need some time to acquire additional models.

MUYBRIDGE
I have a letter I received; it's right here. (*pulling out the letter
from the orphanage and then quickly putting it back*) No, this is
not it. (*continuing to shuffle papers*) Rather, *here* it is. Permission
to photograph some patients from Blockley Hospital, the asylum
across the road. They must be included in our lexicon. We cannot
know normal without abnormal. Yes? For this is not about pretty
pictures on a wheel – and only my photographs provide objective
understanding. We must be unapologetic in our search for truth.

   *He hands TADD the letter and motions for him to go before
   turning to the rest.*

MUYBRIDGE
I want to keep thinking like this, to see things that can illuminate some
of the dark mysteries around us.

   *MUYBRIDGE exits into the darkroom tent as BLANCHE and
   BELL exchange glances.*

   *A motion study begins as the scene shifts. Two nude figures
   exhibit qualities of "abnormal movement."*

[81]

Sound of a horse and carriage coming to a stop. FLORA and LARKYNS walk up the steps to her home. They pause at the threshold. An awkward, adolescent moment of how to say goodbye. Finally he tips his hat and starts to back away. She stops him. Opens her mouth to speak, but can't find any words. He takes out his watch, checks it, and winces as if to say, "It's late!" She takes it from him and looks at it. A naughty look of disbelief as if to say, "I'm in for it now!" She shakes her head.

FLORA

There's no way that watch can be right.

She starts to adjust the time on his watch.

LARKYNS
(*whispers*) What are you doing?

FLORA
(*whispers*) This is more like it.

LARKYNS
(*whispers*) That won't change the fact that it's late.

FLORA
(*whispers*) Shh. Now, don't want it to run slow.

She winds the watch, delicately rolling the mechanism back and forth between her fingertips. He watches intently, aroused. She keeps winding as they look into each other's eyes. They drift closer together. Their lips are nearly touching.

LARKYNS
(*whispers*) Don't overwind it; you'll pop the spring.

She keeps winding. She kisses him. The sound of a tiny "pop."

FLORA
(*whispers*) Oops.

A sound separates them. She drops his watch, which then hangs by his crotch swinging from the watch fob. A shaft of light sweeps across them as MUYBRIDGE steps out of the house. He's about to speak when FLORA attacks.

FLORA
You owe Mr. Larkyns an apology.

MUYBRIDGE
	What?

FLORA
	I tore my dress, because it's shoddy. He was humiliated.
	I was humiliated. I need new clothes.

MUYBRIDGE
	Do you know what time it is?

FLORA
	I do because I just asked. It's a quarter of midnight.

MUYBRIDGE
	It's two thirty.

FLORA
	Not according to his watch. Goodnight, sir. I'm very sorry for
	your troubles.

		*She passes MUYBRIDGE and heads inside leaving LARKYNS
		standing awkwardly on the doorstep.*

LARKYNS
	No trouble really. The dress ... I didn't even notice.

		*MUYBRIDGE reaches down and grabs LARKYNS's watch,
		glances at it, then stares into LARKYNS's eyes.*

LARKYNS
	It's not the most reliable timepiece. Americans haven't yet
	learned how to –

		*MUYBRIDGE violently rips the watch from LARKYNS's vest
		and clutches it in his fist.*

MUYBRIDGE
	Stay away from my wife.

LARKYNS
	Oh, you've got it all wrong. my man.

MUYBRIDGE
	If I ever see you again, I assure you it will be for the last time.
	Do you understand?

LARKYNS
	You needn't –

MUYBRIDGE
Do you understand?

Pause.

LARKYNS
I would never want to be the cause of such a misunderstanding
between a husband and his wife. So with all due respect, I will
take my leave.

LARKYNS stands waiting. MUYBRIDGE doesn't move.

LARKYNS
My watch?

*Again MUYBRIDGE doesn't move, but continues to grip the
watch in his fist.*

LARKYNS
You know what? It's yours. A gift. A gentlemen's understanding.
I fear it's broken though. I'm quite certain there's no way it can
be before midnight.

MUYBRIDGE
A watch can be repaired.

LARKYNS
Indeed.

He tips his hat, spins on his heel, and walks off.

CAMERA OBSCURA
||||||||||||||||||||||||||||||||||||||||||||||||||||||

Darkness. Sound of chemicals.

*Projection (image): A woman with her body contorted
in the throes of a seizure*

BLANCHE
When you look at all of these pictures, what do you think?

BELL
I think that's a lot of pictures. How about you?

BLANCHE
I first thought he's trying to show us something.

BELL
And now?

BLANCHE

Now I think he's trying to find something.

BELL

Yes.

BLANCHE

And we're all searching with him.

BELL

Feeling our way in the dark.

Contact between them.

MUYBRIDGE

(*offstage*) Clear to enter?

BLANCHE

Yes.

BELL

No. I mean, yes, now.

MUYBRIDGE enters.

MUYBRIDGE

Bell, are you finished preparing those plates?

BELL

Yes.

MUYBRIDGE

Well then, can you load the cameras? Time. Time is our enemy.

BELL exits. BLANCHE shows MUYBRIDGE some notes.

BLANCHE

Here are a few suggestions.

MUYBRIDGE

Let's see. (*looks at her list*) There's a lot of objects: handkerchiefs, cigarettes, brushes ...

BLANCHE

They help tell the story.

MUYBRIDGE

I'm not interested in scenarios, just actions.

BLANCHE

Um ... (*referring to the developed plates*) What do I call these in the catalogue?

MUYBRIDGE

"Artificially Induced Convulsions."

BLANCHE

Artificially induced?

MUYBRIDGE

The model volunteered to receive an electric current though her skin. Her muscles were forced into a sort of seizure.

BLANCHE

Was it painful?

MUYBRIDGE

It shouldn't be. On paper it's painless. But she's not coming back. We just wanted an investigation of the body acting without any will or control.

> *BLANCHE is scrutinizing the photograph.*

BLANCHE

Oh, like being possessed.

> *MUYBRIDGE reaches out towards her as if to touch her. Just before he makes contact a noise is heard outside the tent. He pulls away as RONDINELLA enters.*

RONDINELLA

Sir?

MUYBRIDGE

What is it?

RONDINELLA

I found your subject.

MUYBRIDGE

Subject?

RONDINELLA

(*touches chest*) Thump-thump, thump-thump.

MUYBRIDGE

Yes? Let's see.

> *RONDINELLA exits followed by MUYBRIDGE. BLANCHE stares at the photos of the woman for a moment and then decides to follow.*

*In the photography compound, MUYBRIDGE, RONDINELLA,
BELL, BIGLER, TADD, and BLANCHE have gathered around a
crate that's on a rolling cart positioned underneath a battery
of cameras. Inside the crate is the animal that will provide the
subject for their beating-heart series. Out of sight from the
audience, a battery of cameras is positioned above the crate with
the lenses pointing down towards the ground. RONDINELLA is
adjusting the placement of the cart to line up with the lenses.
MUYBRIDGE is working the angle of the lid to see if he can reflect
any more light into the crate. BELL is holding a rope attached to
the cart and is standing by to pull the cart slowly down the track.
BIGLER is kneeling by the crate attempting to feed a blade of grass
to the animal inside. TADD stands holding a knife.*

BIGLER
Should we turn the turtle on its front?

RONDINELLA
I think you're missing the point, Bigler.

MUYBRIDGE
Bigler.

BIGLER
Sorry. Just wanted him to be comfortable.

MUYBRIDGE
Are we ready?

BIGLER
I just want to say, I / don't feel –

RONDINELLA
Cameras are set.

BELL
Better be. All or nothing with this one.

MUYBRIDGE
Mr. Tadd.

TADD hands MUYBRIDGE the knife.

MUYBRIDGE
Standing by. On my mark.

He positions the knife inside the crate. BLANCHE strains to see.
BIGLER turns away with his hands on the switch of the timing
mechanism.

MUYBRIDGE
Don't block the light. Three, two, one ...

He slices down the length of the animal.

MUYBRIDGE
Wait. Mr. Tadd.

TADD reaches in and helps MUYBRIDGE open up the animal to
reveal the heart.

MUYBRIDGE
Come on, come on, where are you ... There!

The group gasps at the sight of the beating heart. Even BIGLER,
despite himself, glances back to see.

MUYBRIDGE
Go! Now! Mark!

BELL pulls the cart slowly down the track and the cameras fire.

BIGLER
Uh, one Londonderry, two Londonderry, three Londonderry. Complete.

A cheer. Then an awkward pause as they stand watching
the dying animal. People slowly pull back and walk away
as the scene shifts.

WITH CHILD
||||||||||||||||||||||||||||||

MUYBRIDGE sets the knife aside and reaches into the crate.
FLORA enters and finds MUYBRIDGE rummaging through it.

FLORA
What are you doing?

MUYBRIDGE pulls out a dress.

MUYBRIDGE
Are you packing?

She picks up the knife in disbelief.

FLORA
You broke open the lock?

[88]

MUYBRIDGE
Are you planning a trip?

FLORA
This is mine!

MUYBRIDGE
Answer me!

FLORA
You don't trust me.

MUYBRIDGE
You've packed a box full of your clothes. What am I to think?

FLORA
That I'm running away?

MUYBRIDGE
Don't think for a second that I won't –

FLORA
Maybe I should. Maybe I should go. Rather than live like this. Under your constant stare. Day, middle of the night, I wake up and find / you hovering over my bed.

MUYBRIDGE
(*thrusting the dress towards her*) For good reason it seems! Where were you planning to go?

FLORA
I'm pregnant!

> *Beat.*

FLORA
I was packing up the things that wouldn't fit anymore. Thought we could start fresh. But I suppose my mistakes will always hang around my neck. I suppose forgiveness is impossible with you. Why do you worry if I run away? Why don't you just make me leave if you despise me so?

MUYBRIDGE
Flora.

> *He holds her. Touches her belly.*

MUYBRIDGE
Flora. My Flora.

> *He holds her. Then, almost as ritual, replaces the dress in the crate and drags it offstage.*

MUYBRIDGE

The past is past. And I blow it away. Whoosh ... whoosh ... whoosh ...

She smiles as he goes. After a beat, FLORA falls to the ground and weeps.

MISSING PICTURES
llllllllllllllllllllllllllllllllllllllllllllll

Compound, morning. MUYBRIDGE enters from the tent with a set of plates.

MUYBRIDGE

Good morning, team. Gather round!

RONDINELLA

Are those the turtle?

The group gathers around MUYBRIDGE, who unveils the glass plate and holds it high above his head towards the sun. Everyone stares up at it.

MUYBRIDGE

Two complete contractions of the heart.

BIGLER

And everything moves around it.

MUYBRIDGE

Yes, a sympathetic action.

The group gazes in reverence.

BLANCHE

Last night I had a dream where I watched these pictures being taken again. But, then, in the middle of it all, I became the turtle. Or rather I lay on top of the turtle's back. (*touching MUYBRIDGE*) And you ... took a knife and said, "This is for the future." And the cameras clicked. And I could see the photographs instantaneously. A little red ball, squeezed by an invisible fist.

MUYBRIDGE stares at her, as does the rest of the group. An awkward silence. BELL breaks the tension.

BELL

Will you marry me?

Laughter.

RONDINELLA
A darkroom technician? He'll be blind before he's thirty. I on the other hand have a very bright future.

SUSAN
Don't be silly. (*referring to BLANCHE*) We're going to be old maids together and love it!

BIGLER
Oh.

MUYBRIDGE
Mr. Bell, apologize immediately.

BELL
For what?

MUYBRIDGE
Your lack of decorum. I think it's obvious. There's no room for fraternizing with models.

BELL
She's not a model.

MUYBRIDGE
Staff. Anybody. We're working here!

BELL
I was just teasing.

MUYBRIDGE
Then get back to work!

>   *PEPPER and EAKINS enter.*

PEPPER
Muybridge!

MUYBRIDGE
Dr. Pepper. Eakins.

EAKINS
Ed.

PEPPER
It's over! It's over! The veterinary school is incensed. Claim you stole a turtle and killed it.

MUYBRIDGE
I –

PEPPER

It was apparently a hundred years old! Had become a bit of mascot.

MUYBRIDGE

Oh.

EAKINS

My God. Is this it?

MUYBRIDGE

I wasn't aware –

EAKINS

It's beautiful. Extraordinary.

PEPPER

Yes?

EAKINS

Oh Billy, it's like a musical coda at the end of the work. All of this movement, all of these animals, and the end: this beating heart concludes the story. Heartbreaking.

PEPPER

Huh. Well, there's the artist at work. All right, I'll handle the vets. Well done, Muybridge. The jewel in the crown. Let's get printing.

MUYBRIDGE

Printing? No, we're not done.

PEPPER

Of course we are.

MUYBRIDGE

But don't you see some new potential with this?

PEPPER

Muybridge! We're out of money, out of time. Subscribers are cancelling. I've asked Eakins to help you create the galley proofs for the publication.

MUYBRIDGE

I don't need help.

PEPPER

Or he can do it alone.

MUYBRIDGE

I –

PEPPER

    Good. Then if there's nothing else left to capture,
I'll congratulate you all –

BLANCHE

    Mother and child.

PEPPER

    What?

BLANCHE

    We haven't got any of children. It's been especially requested.

PEPPER

    Muybridge?

BLANCHE

    Children are all of our pasts. We have to look there to understand our
present movement. Our future movement.

    Beat.

MUYBRIDGE

    Indeed.

PEPPER

    Very well. You've got tomorrow and then we wrap up the project. And
Muybridge, the work is good, it's yours, be happy it's done.

    PEPPER and EAKINS exit.

MUYBRIDGE

    Well? Mother and child. Tadd?

TADD

    I have a toddler and a baby boy. But my wife would never pose.

SUSAN

    I could it do it. After this heals.

MUYBRIDGE

    We only have tomorrow.

RONDINELLA

    Maybe pirate and child.

MUYBRIDGE

    Would you be able to, Blanche?

BELL

    She's not a model.

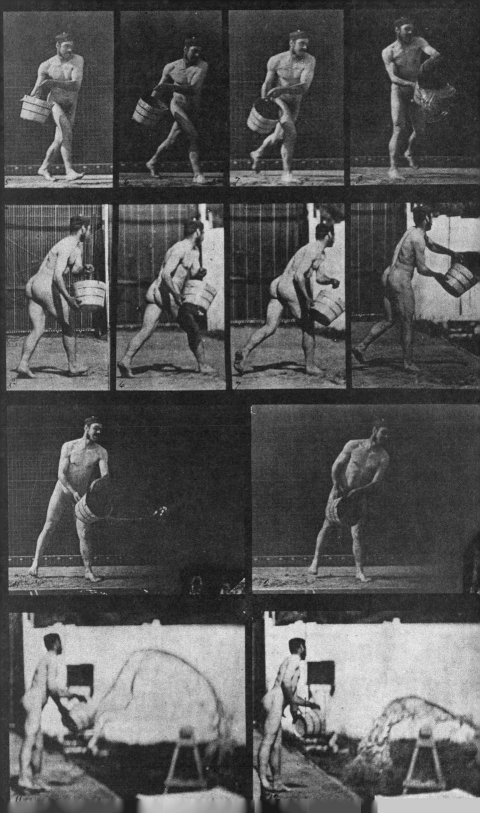

MUYBRIDGE
Just for this one? It would help me.

BLANCHE
I suppose you'd need it without clothes.

MUYBRIDGE
If you're comfortable.

BELL
She's not.

MUYBRIDGE
This doesn't concern you, Mr. Bell.

BELL
But –

MUYBRIDGE
You have some plates to prepare.

BELL
Sir.

He exits into the tent. The rest of the team quietly slips out.

BLANCHE
I don't know if –

MUYBRIDGE
When all this is long past the only thing that will be revealed about you will be that you were a participant in an investigation – a woman simply trying to understand as much as she could about the world.

He exits leaving her to think. BLANCHE looks at the bucket sitting on the stage. Projections of images featuring this prop appear above her.

Projection (image): A woman carries the bucket up an incline plane

Projection (image): A man empties water from the bucket

Projection (image): A woman empties water from the bucket

Projection (image): A woman carries the bucket up a set of stairs

Projection (image): A woman pours water from the bucket onto another woman

BLANCHE, focusing intently on her action, picks up the bucket, walks with it a few steps, and places it down. MUYBRIDGE returns and watches her intently. BLANCHE places the bucket down and walks away.

> *FLORA enters, visibly pregnant. She walks to the bucket, kneels down, and throws up. MUYBRIDGE watches her helplessly.*

MUYBRIDGE
Are you ready for the picture?

FLORA
I hate my body!

> *FLORA throws up.*

MUYBRIDGE
Oh, poor thing.

> *She retches again. He picks up a pear that rests on top of the camera.*

MUYBRIDGE
Would a pear help?

> *She takes it, throws it at him. Retches again.*

MUYBRIDGE
Well, I have the camera set up.

FLORA
I should weigh twenty pounds, but I'm fat and hideous and disgusting.

> *He bends down to her and holds her.*

MUYBRIDGE
You're beautiful – the most beautiful thing I've ever seen. You're glowing with the –

> *She retches again.*

FLORA
Jesus!

MUYBRIDGE
(*admonishing*) Flora.

FLORA
I can't take it –

MUYBRIDGE
I just want to take a simple picture – it's not hard.

FLORA
I don't want to.

MUYBRIDGE

What do you mean you don't want to? I had a bough of pears
delivered to the studio.

FLORA

Why did you waste money on pears? I hate pears.

MUYBRIDGE

Well, they're a symbol. Of fertility.

FLORA

You know, I'm not really in the mood to be a symbol.

MUYBRIDGE

You just have to be yourself – and the camera will do the rest.
Please. Flora.

FLORA

If I can have money for the circus?

MUYBRIDGE

The circus?

FLORA

One last outing.

MUYBRIDGE

I can't, Flora. I have the commission with Leland Stanford.

FLORA

I can go with the church ladies.

MUYBRIDGE

It doesn't seem very proper to be out in public like this.

FLORA

You're worried I'll join the freak show.

MUYBRIDGE

No, I'm not ... I'm not worried. You can go to the circus.

FLORA

Good, I'll bring you home a treat!

MUYBRIDGE

All I want is to capture you just like this.

She smiles and poses for him.

MUYBRIDGE

Thank you. It's for the baby. When it's older. To understand.
The beauty of where it came from. The art in its life.

DELIVERY
IIIIIIIIIIIIIIIIIIIIIIIII

> *A thundering knock at a door. A lone woman, MRS. SMITH,
> a nurse, scuttles slowly down the stage. Thunderous knocking
> continues.*

MRS. SMITH

Who's there?

> *Voices – an inhuman sound. More pounding. A shaft of light as
> the door swings open.*

MRS. SMITH

Mary and Joseph.

> *LARKYNS staggers in with FLORA in his arms; she's in labour.*

LARKYNS

Help.

MRS. SMITH

Henry?

> *LARKYNS makes unintelligible sounds which may be an attempt
> to say, "I didn't know she had such a fear of tigers." He panics.*

MRS. SMITH

This woman is having a baby!

> *More noises from LARKYNS that sound like "It's a circus.
> After all, she wanted to go."*

MRS. SMITH

Where did you find her?

> *More noises from LARKYNS that sound like "I'm not normally
> on this end of the operation."*

MRS. SMITH

Is she yours? Henry, did you ...? When did you ...?

LARKYNS

Can we talk about this later?!

MRS. SMITH
  Bring her in here. There, there, love, we'll take care of you.

FLORA
  Henry?

        MRS. SMITH takes FLORA away. LARKYNS starts checking his
        clothes. He frantically wipes at them, straightens them, then takes
        off his jacket and shakes it out. MRS. SMITH comes back.

MRS. SMITH
  Who is this girl?

LARKYNS
  I think I sat in taffy. Can you help me?

MRS. SMITH
  She has a wedding ring on.

        LARKYNS checks his trousers.

LARKYNS
  It's everywhere.

        He takes his trousers off.

MRS. SMITH
  She's not your wife.

LARKYNS
  Strangest thing.

MRS. SMITH
  Why are you with her?

        LARKYNS takes off his shirt.

LARKYNS
  I have to get cleaned up. I've missed the laundry. Can you help?

MRS. SMITH
  Yes, I'll help her. But I think you're in trouble.

LARKYNS
  Nothing that a good pressing won't take care of.

        LARKYNS continues to strip.

MRS. SMITH
  Wait here.

LARKYNS
I might have to step out to Chinatown. Otherwise, I'll be around.

MRS. SMITH
Henry, where's her husband?

> *There's a cry from offstage. MRS. SMITH exits. LARKYNS, now naked, walks upstage.*

LARKYNS
It's horrible. It's like an animal. Like some wild beast. Like some crazed animal. Mrs. Smith, I've seen a lot of things, but I ... this was an animal wearing a lady's dress. And full of blood.

> *He steps through the door and suddenly LARKYNS runs full out – though not covering any ground. His action transforms into a motion study as the scene shifts.*

MOTHER AND CHILD

> *In the photography compound, a male model runs naked as the cameras fire. PEPPER watches with the crew. He checks his watch.*

BIGLER
Complete!

TADD
(*to model*) Looked good. Thanks for coming in.

> *The model exits, passing SUSAN as she enters. There's a fast reset of the cameras.*

MUYBRIDGE
We're going to have to maximize the available light. Reverse the position of the foreshortening.

RONDINELLA
Got it.

TADD
We've got the models ready. Two toddlers, a couple of older boys, an infant, a woman to play the mother.

SUSAN
There are two toddlers?

> *SUSAN quickly exits.*

MUYBRIDGE

Good, have them stand by and I'll take the exposed plates in.

MUYBRIDGE exits. The men scramble into action.
BLANCHE enters wearing a model's gown.

BELL

What are you doing?

BLANCHE

Mother and child.

BELL

Why?

BIGLER

(*squeezing by*) Excuse me, sorry.

BLANCHE

They need a model.

BELL

Tadd found one.

BLANCHE

I want to model.

BELL

You don't want to be seen by all these guys.

BLANCHE

They never pay any mind. "In front of the cameras we're just another / animal."

BELL

Everybody sees everything.

RONDINELLA

(*yelling to TADD*) You're going to have to go farther back.

BLANCHE

There's so many pictures. So many! In the future no one will see me or you or any one person, just the movement.

BELL

Really? Why do you think he takes so many pictures of women?

BLANCHE

No. Same as for men. Just examples.

BELL

Or maybe ...?

BLANCHE

I suggested the mother and child study to him.

BELL

Well, I suppose you've got a hold on him.

BLANCHE

No. Just –

BELL

And I think he wants a hold on you. (*gesturing*) And soon you'll be this big by this big.

BLANCHE

He's got pictures of you.

BELL

Not anymore. I asked him not to publish them. I thought you'd like that.

BLANCHE

I liked that you modelled. That you were free to do that. And I thought you'd feel the same.

BELL

No. Don't you see what he's doing? He wants to own you forever.

BLANCHE

And you don't want him to.

BELL

No.

BLANCHE

Why?

BELL

Because ...

BLANCHE

Maybe *you'd* prefer to own me?

> BIGLER *passes by attempting to be inconspicuous.*

BELL

Well, what do you prefer?

BLANCHE

To do what I want. And you should keep your eyes to yourself.

BELL

Fine. I'll still see you in the darkroom.

BLANCHE

No, you'll see a piece of paper. But you won't ever see me.

She walks away.

BELL

True, but what's so special about you anyhow? Just another animal.

MUYBRIDGE enters, stops when he sees BLANCHE in her gown.

MUYBRIDGE

(*to TADD*) What's this one's number?

TADD

Uh ...

MUYBRIDGE

Number!

TADD

Say ... thirty-five.

BLANCHE

What's the first series?

MUYBRIDGE is silent.

BLANCHE

Sir.

MUYBRIDGE

Uh ...

He looks around helplessly.

BLANCHE

The first series is woman carrying and rocking infant.

MUYBRIDGE remains unable to speak.

BLANCHE

The action will be approximately three seconds. Set the chronograph to four seventy.

BIGLER

Four seventy, Miss.

BLANCHE
  The model is number thirty-five.

TADD
  Thirty-five.

BLANCHE
  The costume is ... nude. Susan.

  SUSAN enters with the baby.

BLANCHE
  Standing by.

  *The men are behind the cameras. MUYBRIDGE still stands
  motionless just off the track. BLANCHE looks to BELL; he nods
  and turns his back. The other men look respectfully away from
  her and towards their work.*

RONDINELLA
  Standing by, Miss.

  *MUYBRIDGE stares at BLANCHE, who confidently disrobes and
  receives the baby from SUSAN, who picks up BLANCHE's gown
  and clears the frame.*

BLANCHE
  On your mark.

RONDINELLA
  Three, two, one ... mark.

  *She walks towards MUYBRIDGE gently cradling the baby and
  rocking it gently.*

BLANCHE
  (*as she walks*) There, there. Your mommy isn't far away. Hush.

BIGLER
  Complete!

  *SUSAN rushes in with her gown. BLANCHE stands and hands
  the baby to MUYBRIDGE so that she can receive her gown.
  Upon contact with the baby, MUYBRIDGE is overwhelmed,
  thrown into crisis, and the photography compound dissolves
  as MRS. SMITH enters carrying a letter which she holds in
  front of MUYBRIDGE to read.*

CHANGELING
|||||||||||||||||||||||||||||||||||||||||

> *MUYBRIDGE holds his baby.*

MRS. SMITH
I've passed letters between your wife and Mr. Larkyns for months.

> *MUYBRIDGE hands the baby to MRS. SMITH and reads the letter.*

MUYBRIDGE
Come with me.

> *They enter FLORA's room. FLORA quickly hides something behind her back.*

FLORA
I said I'm sick and I need quiet.

> *MUYBRIDGE grabs the object, a photograph, from her.*

MUYBRIDGE
What is this?

FLORA
What?

MUYBRIDGE
What is this? This!

FLORA
Just a picture of the baby.

MUYBRIDGE
I've never seen this picture before.

> *MUYBRIDGE examines it closely. She tries to grab it back but he pulls it away.*

FLORA
I wanted a keepsake ... that's all.

> *Feels the paper. Turns it over.*

MUYBRIDGE
What's this? "Little Henry."

> *FLORA is silent.*

MUYBRIDGE
Your handwriting.

FLORA

(*quietly*) Let me go.

MUYBRIDGE

My baby. My baby is gone.

MRS. SMITH

No, he's right here, sir.

MUYBRIDGE

My boy is gone and a monster has taken his place.

FLORA

Then let us go.

MRS. SMITH

Now, sir, remember, he's just a child. He can't be blamed for the faults of others.

> *MUYBRIDGE looks at a bunch of photos. He's panicking.*

MUYBRIDGE

He's not here. He's not here. He's not here. (*looking at the baby*) He's not here. How do you get rid of it?

FLORA

No!

MRS. SMITH

You can't get rid of it. It's a baby.

MUYBRIDGE

It's a changeling. How do you get rid of a changeling?

MRS. SMITH

Maybe sit down.

FLORA

Please let us go!

MUYBRIDGE

My baby!

> *He freaks out rushing at FLORA as though he's going to tear her apart as well. She screams and he suddenly grows very calm. She looks up at him and he's gazing off into space.*

MUYBRIDGE

You see, I simply thought it was my baby.

MRS. SMITH
It's your baby – it *is* your baby. And *your* baby. Together.

MUYBRIDGE
May I see that letter from Mr. Larkyns? Please.

MRS. SMITH
All right.

She hands him the letter.

MUYBRIDGE
No, I'm sorry, I meant the envelope. I'd like to see the return address.

She hands him the envelope – then instantly wishes she hadn't.

MRS. SMITH
Now, sir ...

MUYBRIDGE
Thank you. You've been of extraordinary value to me.

*He starts emptying his pockets of money and giving it to her.
Bills, coins, a ring.*

FLORA
What are you doing?

MRS. SMITH
Please don't.

MUYBRIDGE
It's a bonus.

MRS. SMITH
No, sir. I never meant.

FLORA
No!

The scene shifts.

THE WITNESS
||||||||||||||||||||||||||||||||||||

*At the murder trial of MUYBRIDGE, his old associate, RULOFSON,
testifies as to what he remembers of the day of the murder. He
holds his right hand on the Bible.*

RULOFSON

And nothing but the truth, so help me God. I saw him in the elevator
at my office on the seventeenth. He was white as marble and his lips
compressed. I asked him what was the matter; his answer was –

MUYBRIDGE shakes convulsively.

RULOFSON

I believed he had gone mad. Tears and perspiration streamed
down his face.

MUYBRIDGE

My poor wife, what will become of her? Make me a promise to settle my
business with my wife the same as with me.

RULOFSON

He said he had no thought of suicide /

MUYBRIDGE

It's my honour I want to vindicate and in doing so –

RULOFSON

but that he might lose his life. I argued with him for an hour refusing
to let him go until he told me what had happened between his wife and
Mr. Larkyns. He said that Mr. Larkyns was –

MUYBRIDGE

– hiding at the Yellow Jacket Mine near Calistoga.

RULOFSON

And that he needed to catch the boat across the bay.

MUYBRIDGE

Look at the time. I've got to go.

MUYBRIDGE is pushing forward to get on his way.
RULOFSON is backpedalling, pleading with MUYBRIDGE.

RULOFSON

I tried to talk some more against time, as I knew the boat left at
four o'clock.

MUYBRIDGE tears away from him.

RULOFSON

It was four minutes to four when he left my office; my office is twelve
blocks from the boat – ten minutes' walk for me. My watch was very
near city time.

A boat's horn blows. MUYBRIDGE is gone.

CRIB PLAYER ONE and CRIB PLAYER TWO take the stand.

CRIB PLAYER ONE
On the night of the seventeenth, as I remember, we were engaged in a
friendly game of cribbage.

CRIB PLAYER TWO
On that night we were engaged in a vicious game of cribbage.

CRIB PLAYER ONE
A friendly vicious game of cribbage.

CRIB PLAYER TWO
It was the kind of night you could hear for miles.

CRIB PLAYER ONE
A horse and carriage.

CRIB PLAYER TWO
Footsteps approaching from the gate a half-mile down the hill.

MUYBRIDGE is revealed, walking slowly, intently.

CRIB PLAYER ONE
It was the kind of night you couldn't trust yourself to behave.

CRIB PLAYER TWO
To control your emotions.

CRIB PLAYER ONE
I could see myself kissing another man.

CRIB PLAYER TWO
I could see this man kissing plenty of others.

CRIB PLAYER ONE
Me too.

CRIB PLAYER TWO
Add me to his list.

CRIB PLAYER ONE
Me too.

MUYBRIDGE continues to walk.

CRIB PLAYER TWO
We were telling stories.

CRIB PLAYER ONE
Anecdotes.

CRIB PLAYER TWO
Rumours.

CRIB PLAYER ONE
Henry had a few.

CRIB PLAYER TWO
A few too many.

CRIB PLAYER ONE
We all had.

CRIB PLAYER TWO
Henry had a son.

CRIB PLAYER ONE
By the wife of a photographer.

CRIB PLAYER TWO
He had eighty-eight points.

CRIB PLAYER ONE
And it was his crib.

CRIB PLAYER TWO
I had counted.

CRIB PLAYER ONE
So had I.

CRIB PLAYER TWO
Henry was about to.

> MUYBRIDGE *arrives at the door of the house. Three knocks are heard. Knock, knock, knock.*

CRIB PLAYER ONE
When a knock came at the door.

> *Knock, knock, knock.*

CRIB PLAYER TWO
And Mr. Stuart, who owned the house, said –

> *Knock, knock, knock.*

CRIB PLAYER ONE
Hey, Larkyns, it's for you.

LARKYNS approaches the door and looks out. MUYBRIDGE
is in the shadows. The ensemble has assembled behind him.
Each holds a pistol.

LARKYNS
Yes?

MUYBRIDGE
Mr. Larkyns?

LARKYNS
Who is that? Dark as pitch out here.

CRIB PLAYER ONE
I admit that later that night I peeked at Larkyns's crib. Six, seven, eight,
and nine. The upturned card was a seven. Thus, he had eight points
for straights, six for fifteens, and two for a pair making sixteen. Very
nice crib.

LARKYNS
I'm in the middle of a game – who is it?

MUYBRIDGE
My name is Muybridge. I have a message for you, from my wife.

A line of hands each holding a gun enters the light.
MUYBRIDGE shoots LARKYNS.

A motion study begins. The gun recoils; LARKYNS's body folds,
receiving the impact of the bullet.

LARKYNS looks up.

LARKYNS
She said that did she? You're sure you're not paraphrasing or
something?

MUYBRIDGE
Mr. Larkyns then proceeded on the following journey demonstrating
several common types of animal locomotion.

The ensemble act out LARKYNS's movement. They proceed
through MUYBRIDGE's description of each phase of his journey.

MUYBRIDGE
He "ambled" back to the living room. Then "meandered" through the
kitchen. Next he "sashayed" out the rear door.

The scene shifts as the ensemble now witness LARKYNS's final steps.

MUYBRIDGE
At last he "sauntered," "moseyed," and "shimmied" to the oak tree.

LARKYNS winds through the crowd.

MUYBRIDGE
There he "teetered," "swaggered," "faltered," "staggered," "stumbled," and at last somewhat gracefully "reclined." And died. As all animals eventually do in one way or another.

With a sigh, LARKYNS expires. The ensemble gathers around the body and then looks back to the figure of MUYBRIDGE, who stands with his smoking gun.

MUYBRIDGE
I do remember the first time I saw Flora quite distinctly.

FLORA enters, reprising her first appearance at Muybridge's studio. In an instant, she is gone.

MUYBRIDGE
I can't say that I can remember the last time I saw her.

The scene shifts as the ensemble transforms into the jury.

VERDICT

The ensemble assemble into an orderly formation of the jury. MUYBRIDGE stands awaiting his verdict. The JURY FOREMAN steps forward.

JURY FOREMAN
Yes, Your Honour, we have reached a unanimous verdict.

MUYBRIDGE stands in helpless resignation.

JURY FOREMAN
We unanimously reject the defence of "not guilty by reason of insanity" as all evidence points to a man who was clear thinking and acting in an obviously premeditated fashion. This was a man who, while in complete control of his actions, made the choice to execute Henry Larkyns.

MUYBRIDGE stands still, staring at the JURY FOREMAN.

JURY FOREMAN
Henry Larkyns, the lying, cheating, philandering seducer, who stole the heart of this man's wife and defiled their marriage –

Goddammit, Your Honour – I would have shot the son of a bitch myself. So to the charge of murder, we find the defendant not guilty by reason of doing the right thing. Good on ya, man.

> *A gavel strikes.*

LAST STUDY
‖‖‖‖‖‖‖‖‖‖‖‖‖‖‖‖‖‖‖‖‖‖‖‖‖‖‖‖

> *MUYBRIDGE and BLANCHE stand side by side reviewing the completed catalogue.*

MUYBRIDGE
I didn't expect to live.

BLANCHE
And then you were free.

MUYBRIDGE
Or rather sentenced to life.

BLANCHE
And your wife.

MUYBRIDGE
I never saw her again. She died shortly afterwards.

BLANCHE
How?

MUYBRIDGE
Heartbreak I suppose.

BLANCHE
Oh. And the baby?

MUYBRIDGE
Orphanage.

> *Shows picture.*

BLANCHE
He has your eyes.

MUYBRIDGE
"Little Henry."

BLANCHE
Maybe your wife saw what she wanted to see.

MUYBRIDGE
He was better off there.

BLANCHE
But all alone.

MUYBRIDGE
We're all of us alone.

BLANCHE
There's the last set.

Projection (image): A woman lifting a child

MUYBRIDGE
I haven't taken a beautiful photograph for a very long time.
Perhaps the last one was of Flora.

BLANCHE
We completed quite a few series with children and mother and child.
And there's the series Susan wanted.

Projection (image): A failed attempt by a woman to kick a hat and have it land on her head

BLANCHE
That was the best one. I think her eye might have interfered.

MUYBRIDGE
Right. And the series of you?

BLANCHE
I like it. I see myself. And I see I am a different person here, and
here and here and here. And right now, here, I'm different again.
Which means there are so many possibilities. My body is the
riverbank changing slowly over time, but I am the river, entirely
new with each passing moment.

Silence. MUYBRIDGE continues to gaze upon the collected images.

BLANCHE
What will you do now that it's done?

MUYBRIDGE
I don't know.

BLANCHE
Might you still need an assistant?

MUYBRIDGE

I'm not who you think I am. I'm not who you're looking for.

*He feels in his pocket and produces the gun. He contemplates
it for a moment.*

BLANCHE

I don't care about the past.

*MUYBRIDGE removes the bullets. He finds a tool and pries the
lead tip of the bullet from the casing and pours out the gunpowder
onto a tray. BLANCHE watches him.*

BLANCHE

What do you do when everything you think you know is gone?

MUYBRIDGE

You must begin again, starting with looking at the world in those
very small but reliable pieces in hope that over time a new picture
will emerge.

BLANCHE

How?

MUYBRIDGE

Maybe start by walking.

*MUYBRIDGE stops working with the gun and produces a
collection of glass plates.*

MUYBRIDGE

Can you deliver these to Mr. Bell? In appreciation of his work
on the project.

BLANCHE

Mr. Bell?

MUYBRIDGE

Remember: small, reliable pieces.

BLANCHE shakes his hand and starts to leave.

MUYBRIDGE

Before you go ... may I have a photograph of you ... and me?

BLANCHE

There's no light.

MUYBRIDGE sets up one of the cameras and places the tray of gunpowder near it. He takes the timing mechanism and pulls a set of wires and places it into the tray.

MUYBRIDGE

Let's see. The timer will provide a spark and should set off the gunpowder to provide a moment of light. .

BLANCHE

Did you just think of this now?

MUYBRIDGE

No, I read about it somewhere. Pure plagiarism. Stand here with me.

The sound of a ticking clock. MUYBRIDGE and BLANCHE stand stone-still next to each another. A stoic portrait. Then a low roar sounds as if the world has gone into slow motion as the shutter releases and the gunpowder ignites. A pool of light expands from the tray and slowly grows to fill the space. Just before the light hits the pair, they turn and lock eyes as the light washes over them. The light fades and MUYBRIDGE is alone.

FATHER AND SON
||||||||||||||||||||||||||||||||||||||||||||||||

The scene shifts to the orphanage in California. FLOREDO is in the distance, working. MUYBRIDGE stands; he holds the photograph and compares the image to the young man.

MUYBRIDGE

When I arrived at the orphanage I saw a young man doing chores and feeding horses.

MUYBRIDGE walks up to the boy. A very distant train whistle is heard.

MUYBRIDGE

You're a good worker. You're strong for a boy your size.

FLOREDO looks up at MUYBRIDGE and stares at him.

FLOREDO

Yes, Father.

Pause.

MUYBRIDGE

Do you know who I am?

FLOREDO
   Yes.

MUYBRIDGE
   Who am I?

FLOREDO
   You're my father.

MUYBRIDGE
   How do you know?

FLOREDO
   I have a picture.

MUYBRIDGE
   Of course. A picture. And you recognized me?

FLOREDO
   Yes.

MUYBRIDGE
   Who gave you this picture?

FLOREDO
   The sister.

MUYBRIDGE
   And what did she tell you?

FLOREDO
   She told me he was my father. And that he loved me. And that one day
   he would come for me.

MUYBRIDGE
   She did.

FLOREDO
   Yes.

MUYBRIDGE
   And then he produced from his bag an ancient piece of paper folded
   and folded and folded in a series of halves into a very tiny square. When
   opened, the well-worn creases formed a grid of lines across its surface.

     FLOREDO has produced the paper and hands it to MUYBRIDGE.

FLOREDO
   (*pointing at the image*) There you are.

     A long pause as MUYBRIDGE takes in the picture.

MUYBRIDGE

It was a page from a children's illustrated Bible, depicting the image of God. An old man, with white hair and flowing white beard, with stern and judging eyes.

FLOREDO

Have you been watching me?

MUYBRIDGE

Hmm?

FLOREDO

The sister says you're always watching.

MUYBRIDGE

Yes.

FLOREDO

I looked for you looking at me. But I couldn't see you.

MUYBRIDGE

That's all right. What makes a man is what he does, not what he sees.

MUYBRIDGE watches FLOREDO finish his work.

MUYBRIDGE

I could see him frozen instant by instant. I could see the "how" of his movements. But I could not see the "why." There would never be enough instances in view to give me that knowledge.

FLOREDO

Have you come for me?

Pause.

MUYBRIDGE

No. Not today. Today I only came to see you. And to tell you that I've arranged for you to have a new home.

FLOREDO

Oh.

MUYBRIDGE

You'll work for a kind family.

FLOREDO

And then you'll come for me?

MUYBRIDGE

You'll be very happy there.

FLOREDO
And then you'll come for me?

> *MUYBRIDGE stops working and reaches into his pocket.*
> *A stagecoach can be heard approaching.*

MUYBRIDGE
Do you like horses?

FLOREDO
I do.

MUYBRIDGE
Here's one jumping.

> *MUYBRIDGE hands FLOREDO a flipbook and demonstrates it.*

FLOREDO
Did you make this for me?

MUYBRIDGE
I did.

> *FLOREDO flips the pages again and again. The stagecoach arrives*
> *pulled by a team of horses. MUYBRIDGE takes FLOREDO by the*
> *hand and guides him up to the waiting coach.*

> *He turns to FLOREDO.*

MUYBRIDGE
It's a five-hour journey to the farm.

FLOREDO
How long is that?

MUYBRIDGE
Have you a watch?

FLOREDO
No.

> *MUYBRIDGE reaches in his pocket and pulls out a pocket watch,*
> *he checks the time, then hands it to FLOREDO.*

MUYBRIDGE
For you. You can tell people it belonged to your father. A remembrance.
Take care of it.

> *He presses it into FLOREDO's palm. FLOREDO reaches up and*
> *touches MUYBRIDGE's hair.*

FLOREDO
So white.

MUYBRIDGE lets him go.

FLOREDO
Do you still love me?

MUYBRIDGE
Yes.

The stagecoach begins to move away.

FLOREDO
Will you still be watching?

Silence as MUYBRIDGE gazes at the receding stagecoach.

FLOREDO
Will you still be watching?

MUYBRIDGE turns downstage, still silent.

FLOREDO
Will you?

Silence.

FLOREDO
Will you?

*The train passes with a deafening roar, it drowns him out. It fades
and is replaced by the sound of horse hooves and stagecoach wheels.
MUYBRIDGE is washed away by a river of his photographs.*

RIVER OF TIME
||||||||||||||||||||||||||||||||||||

*SUSAN enters, fully dressed and carrying a parasol and an apple.
She stands on the riverbank and looks offstage.*

SUSAN
Oh come on! After all I've done this summer, I think fair's fair. Come
down here!

*RONDINELLA, TADD, BIGLER, and BELL come on, naked and
huddled in a clump trying to cover themselves with a couple
of blankets.*

BIGLER
Aren't you coming in, Miss?

SUSAN
No. I think I'll enjoy the view.

She takes a big bite of apple and nods to the river.

RONDINELLA
Here's to the end of a long, long summer.

BELL
Three, two, one ... mark!

The young men drop the blankets, holler, and jump in.

TADD
Oh, that's cold!

BIGLER
Freezing!

Everyone but BELL scrambles out again and grabs his blanket.

BELL
It's perfect!

RONDINELLA
Bell.

He points. On the other side, BLANCHE is standing on the riverbank. BELL continues to bathe in the river without responding to her presence. The others all discreetly grab their things and head off.

After a moment BLANCHE walks towards the river.

Projection (text): "Walking"

When she reaches the shore he finally turns to her.

Projection (text): "Turning"

She waves. He returns the gesture and then covers his eyes. She takes off her clothes, steps into the river, and wades towards him.

Projection (text): "Crossing"

He drops his hands and the two gaze upon each other, before drifting together into an embrace.

Projection (text): "Ascending"

They are washed with images and then gone.

EPILOGUE

Stepping forward, MUYBRIDGE presents his body of work.

MUYBRIDGE

In the summer of 1886 at the University of Pennsylvania, I, Eadweard Muybridge, completed the most exhaustive investigation into animal locomotion ever known.

Music.

MUYBRIDGE

And for the first time ever, the accurate depiction and replication of linear action over time was created.

Projection (image): Multiple images from Muybridge motion studies

The stage is covered in a blanket of tiny sequential pictures. An enormous sense of volume.

MUYBRIDGE

In the process I took over a hundred thousand photographs depicting seven hundred and eighty-one different sequences of action: walking, ambling, trotting, and galloping. Jumping, lifting, heaving, reclining.

Projection (image): Animals

MUYBRIDGE

The animals studied included horses, mules, oxen, dogs, cats, goats, lions, elephants, buffalo, camels, deer, pigeons, vultures, ostriches, eagles, cranes, and humans.

The ensemble, naked, are assembled onstage.

Lights focus on the men.

MUYBRIDGE

Two hundred and eleven studies of men ...

On the women.

MUYBRIDGE

Three hundred and three of women ...

The ensemble drop to their knees as FLOREDO sprints through the crowd.

MUYBRIDGE
Sixteen of children ...

Lights isolate individual hands.

MUYBRIDGE
Five of a man's isolated hand ...

Disquieting gesture and movement of one isolated body.

MUYBRIDGE
Twenty-seven of women and men exhibiting pathological or abnormal movement.

Lights fade on the ensemble.

MUYBRIDGE
The results I believe will be an invaluable resource to scientists, doctors, artists, dancers, gamblers, lovers, detectives, juries, and very, very old men. These are our investigations. These are our "Studies in Motion."

A sudden flash of light: a stroboscopic effect of the ensemble in motion.

END

ACKNOWLEDGEMENTS

The author would like to acknowledge the support and participation of the following, who made possible the creation and writing of *Studies in Motion*: first, Kim Collier, Jonathon Young, and the cast and artistic team of each production; Cindy Reid, Nathan Medd, Jen Swan, and Electric Company Theatre; Robert Gardiner, Theatre at UBC, and the Social Sciences and Humanities Research Council; Norman Armour and the PuSh International Performing Arts Festival; the British Columbia Arts Council; Vancouver Playhouse, Yukon Arts Centre, Alberta Theatre Projects, and Festival TransAmérique; Michael Clark and Workshop West Theatre; my Edmonton dramaturgical "helper" Jeff Page; Matthew Jocelyn, Canadian Stage Company, and the Citadel Theatre; Karl Siegler, Kevin Williams, Greg Gibson, Ann-Marie Metten, and Les Smith of Talonbooks; the University of Pennsylvania Archives; and Marita Dachsel.

Studies in Motion has now been adapted into a major motion picture by Motion 58 Productions written by Kyle Rideout and Josh Epstein, with the working title *Eadweard*.

Kevin Kerr is a co-founder of Vancouver's Electric Company Theatre, where he has worked as a member of the creative core since 1996. In various roles, including writer, director, actor, designer, and/or producer, he has collaborated on the creation of numerous works such as *Brilliant! The Blinding Enlightenment of Nikola Tesla*, *The Wake*, *The Score*, *Flop*, *The One That Got Away*, *Dona Flor and Her Two Husbands*, *The Fall*, *Palace Grand*, *Tear the Curtain!*, *Initiation Trilogy*, and *You Are Very Star*. Other plays include *Unity (1918)*, *Skydive*, *The Remittance Man*, *Secret World of Og*, and *Spine*. He co-wrote the screen adaptation of *The Score* produced by Screen Siren Pictures for CBC Television and recently wrote dialogue for the National Film Board of Canada's production of Stan Douglas's interactive augmented reality experience *Circa 1948*. Kerr is a four-time recipient of the Jessie Richardson Theatre Award for Outstanding Original Script and received the 2002 Governor General's Literary Award for Drama. He currently teaches in the department of creative writing at the University of Victoria and lives with his partner and poet, Marita Dachsel, and their three children.

PHOTO BY Nancy Lee